STRUCTURED PSYCHOTHERAPY GROUPS FOR SEXUALLY ABUSED CHILDREN AND ADOLESCENTS

Billie Farmer Corder, EdD

Professional Resource Press
Sarasota, Florida

To receive the latest catalog from Professional Resource Press, please
call 1-800-443-3364, fax to 941-343-9201, write to the address below,
or visit out website: http://www.prpress.com

Published by Professional Resource Press
(An imprint of Professional Resource Exchange, Inc.)
Post Office Box 15560
Sarasota, FL 34277-1560

The editorial copywriter for this book was Barbara Landon, the copy editor was Patricia Rockwood, the managing editor was Debbie Fink, the production coordinator was Laurie Girsch, the graphics designer for Part IV was Bob Lefebvre, and Carol Tornatore created the cover.

Library of Congress Cataloging-in-Publication Data

Corder, Billie Farmer, date.
    Structured psychotherapy groups for sexually abused children and adolescents / Billie
Farmer Corder.
      p. cm.
   Includes bibliographical references.
   ISBN 1-56887-058-2 (alk. paper)
   1. Sexually abused children--Rehabilitation. 2. Sexually abused
teenagers--Rehabilitation. 3. Group psychotherapy for children. 4. Group psychotherapy
for teenagers. 5. Sexually abused children--Rehabilitation--Problems, exercises, etc. 6.
Sexually abused teenagers--Rehabilitation--Problems, exercises, etc. 7. Group
psychotherapy for children--Problems, exercises, etc. 8. Group psychotherapy for
teenagers--Problems, exercises, etc. I. Title.

RJ507.S49 C67 2000
618.92'858360651--dc21

                                00-027227

Dedication

This book is dedicated with love and gratitude to my husband, Bob Corder, who has been friend, family, and co-worker for all these years, and to my parents and sister, Lucy, Kenney, and Jean.

Acknowledgments

I would like to express my gratitude and appreciation to my family — Bob Corder, Lucy and Kenney Farmer, and Jean Farmer McCarthy — and to my extended Hawkins and Farmer families for their support and understanding.

I thank my longtime co-worker Reid Whiteside for the valuable contributions he has made to our shared work, and Dr. Tom Haizlip and the staff of the Child Psychiatry Program of Dorothea Dix Hospital for their assistance and encouragement.

Dr. Michael Rutter shared his knowledge on several research projects. His generosity is appreciated. A research grant from the Burroughs Wellcome Research Foundation is gratefully acknowledged. My thanks also to Dr. Peter A. Keller and Barbara Landon for their editorial assistance, and to Debra Fink and members of the staff of Professional Resource Press for their help in preparing this manuscript.

Special gratitude is expressed to all the children and adolescents who participated in the groups I have described, who used the materials and techniques as part of their process of mastery of victimization and trauma, and who taught us a great deal about survival and coping.

Table of Contents

Chapter 4 *(Continued)*

PART III:
The Sessions

PART IV:
Supplemental Material

Introduction

This book represents a distillation of research and clinical work with adolescent and children's therapy groups which spans more than 30 years. The work has been conducted in state mental hospitals, juvenile court settings, mental health centers, group homes, outpatient clinics, county social services settings, outpatient clinics, and private practice. The techniques for structuring psychotherapy groups with sexually abused children and adolescents were developed in response to needs for effective, time-limited therapeutic interventions for this victimized population, and are based on my work with colleagues on trauma, sexual abuse, and the process of mastery by which children handle trauma.

PART I

PSYCHOTHERAPY FOR THE SEXUALLY ABUSED

CHAPTER 1

Theoretical Issues and Approaches

THE EXTENT OF ABUSE

There is no question that the sexual abuse of children, adolescents, and teenagers in our culture represents a cogent challenge to mental health professionals. Sexual abuse of children and adolescents is almost sure to be an issue in professional mental health practice, regardless of the clinician's theoretical orientation or type of workplace. In a climate of diminishing resources for medical and psychological care, it is clear that mental health practitioners must face this issue with responsible, solid techniques. There is a need for cost-effective mental health interventions in the field of treating our sexually abused youth.

Statistics regarding the numbers of victimized children often vary, due in part to differing definitions of sexual abuse and also to our culture's continually changing resources, methods, and facilities for reporting and investigating abuse. What we do know is that sexual abuse exists and that it can drastically alter the way children develop and behave.

A 1981 survey by the National Center for Child Abuse and Neglect reports that 5% of children are sexually abused by an adult who is familiar to them. Finkelhor, Hotaling, and Lewis (1990) estimate that 27% of women and 16% of men may have experienced some form of sexual abuse. Burgess, Groth, and Holmstrom (1978) suggest that, estimating conservatively, one of every five females in our society has suffered sexual abuse. Nasjleti (1980) and Finkelhor (1987) moreover, propose that the abuse of males is quite likely underreported due to reluctance to admit weakness and fear of accusations of homosexuality. The number of victimized children in the United States is staggering when incest, extrafamilial sexual abuse, and unreported incidents of sexual abuse are combined, according to Mayer (1984). In addition to prevention and awareness that will help to reduce these numbers, there is clearly a need for services and interventions that assist those children whose abuse has already been substantiated.

EFFECTS OF SEXUAL ABUSE
ON CHILDREN AND ADOLESCENTS

Many researchers and child development experts have documented the negative effect of sexual abuse on the development and long-term adjustment of children and adolescents. The extent and depth of the effects of abuse appear to be related to several factors, including (a) the length of time over which the abuse was committed (one incident, short-term abuse, or longstanding abuse); (b) the relationship of the abuser to the victim (victimization by a family member or a trusted, family-like figure as opposed to a casual acquaintance or a stranger); (c) whether or not threats, coercion, or additional physical abuse were used; (d) the presence or absence of adult and family support; and (e) the availability of counseling or therapeutic intervention (Mayer, 1984).

Finkelhor and Browne (1986) have proposed that the degree of trauma from abuse is related to the extent of premature sexual stimulation, feelings of powerlessness, stigmatization related to the child's feeling damaged, shamed, and guilty, and feelings of betrayal by a trusted person. Schetky and Green (1988), proposing a more general framework for evaluating the symptoms and extent of abuse, use the following parameters: developmental level and age, duration and frequency of abuse, presence or absence of physical trauma or coercion, strengths and weaknesses within the child's personality prior to abuse, degree of closeness between the child and the abuser, and the family's and society's handling of the issues involved in disclosed abuse.

Terr (1991), who has divided all childhood trauma into two types — Type I (acute, sudden onset) and Type II (longstanding or repeated trauma) — has observed that both types are likely to produce symptoms such as thought suppression, problems in sleeping, hypervigilance and startle responses, regressive behavior, unusual fears and panic, avoidance behaviors, and irritability. Both Types I and II may result in repeated traumatic memories, repetitive behaviors (possibly in attempts to work through the trauma), fears related to the trauma, depression and lack of enjoyment, and changed attitudes about the future and the trustworthiness of others.

In addition to the preceding symptoms, however, children who have experienced longstanding Type II trauma are also more likely to experience psychic numbing (not feeling alive, "forgetting"), self-hypnosis and dissociation ("separating" themselves from their body and their perception of the trauma), and feelings of rage and anger, sometimes turned against themselves (Terr, 1991).

Children who have experienced sexual abuse often resemble those who have been traumatized in other ways. Physical symptoms of sexual abuse often include injuries and irritation to genital and anal areas, urinary tract infections, enlargement of anal and vaginal areas, and pregnancy (Mayer, 1984). Behavioral and emotional symptoms may include those of posttraumatic stress disorder: avoidant behavior, intrusive memories, unusual fears, and so on, but they are also likely to include cognitive distortion (guilt, low self-esteem, hopelessness, self-blame, negative attributions to causes of external events, etc.), altered emotionality (depression, anxiety demonstrated by hypervigilance or unusual fears), or disturbances in relationships (distrust, feelings of isolation, and difficulties with sexual intimacy). Coping/Avoidant behaviors such as dissociative states, substance abuse, and self-injurious behaviors are not unusual, nor are tension-reducing behaviors such as impulsive acting out, developmentally inappropriate sexual behaviors, eating and sleep disorders, and the presence of impaired self-references (failing to establish boundaries and an adequate, internalized sense of self) (Briere & Runtz, 1987).

Even less chronically and severely abused children, according to Sgroi (1982) may suffer from "damaged goods" syndrome, guilt, fear, depression, low self-esteem, poor social skills, and repressed anger and hostility. Sgroi notes that the absence or presence of these symptoms may be crucial in the development of self-mastery and control, independent behavior, and effective decision-making skills.

Long-term effects of sexual abuse often include problems with parenting, sexual dysfunction, and the development of severe personality disorders such as multiple personality disorder. In some instances sexual abuse is also a factor in child molestation behaviors in adulthood (Mayer, 1984).

VULNERABILITY AND MASTERY:
MITIGATING FACTORS

Not all traumatized children respond alike, and not all traumatized children respond with the severe symptoms mentioned earlier. Among the many factors involved in the ability of children to adapt and cope with stress and trauma are their developmental skill level, their relationship to the perpetrator, the severity and chronicity of abuse, and the response of others to disclosure of the abuse. Anthony and Cohler (1987), Pines (1984), and Rutter (1978) have reported early studies of personality traits and environmental factors that appeared to help children cope and succeed despite trauma and/or victimization. These children are often referred to as "invulnerable." They do not exhibit crippling symptoms or severe developmental delays; rather, they display characteristics such as (a) an ability to attract and utilize support from adults around them; (b) social interaction skills for developing friendships and sharing activities with others; (c) the experience of an intense and satisfying creative outlet such as writing, painting, making models, and so forth; (d) the presence of at least one area in which they are recognized as achieving well; (e) a sense of autonomy and an ability to seek out a "private place" within a chaotic environment; and (f) evidence of cognitive mastery, coping skills, cognitive problem-solving skills, or the ability to "relabel" anxiety-provoking elements in their environment (Pines, 1984).

Anthony and Koupernick (1974) described the ability of "invulnerable" children to develop cognitive receptive and representational skills for creating an adequate frame of reference for thinking, conceptualizing, and making directed decisions. Rutter's 1978 studies of children in deprived socio-economic groups noted that the ability of children to cope is also affected by the number of stressors facing them at any given time: for instance, a mother's marital stress or psychiatric disorder, a father's criminal record, or whether a child has been placed in foster or institutional care.

In addition to the degree of severity of environmental factors, it can be assumed that "invulnerable" children are less likely to suffer physical or mental handicaps or to possess characteristics and temperament with some "goodness of fit" with that of their mother or primary caregiver. They are also less likely to have been scapegoated or otherwise selected to serve a deviant family defense mechanism against stress (although in our experience this latter characteristic is typical of many sexually abused children).

All of these concepts — the extent of abuse, the effects of abuse, and the ability of some abused children to cope more effectively than others — must be considered when planning for intervention and treatment for sexually abused children. They are crucial for setting goals and evaluating progress within the treatment process.

CHAPTER 2

Implications for Treatment

Sgroi (1982) has noted that short-term therapy, even for less severely abused children, is often focused on the symptoms that interfere with control and self-mastery. Without adequate mastery skills, he writes, it appears unlikely that effective independent behavior, judgment, and decision-making skills can develop. Sgroi's treatment techniques have included role-modeling, role-playing, peer group support, and structured practice in independent decision making within an accepting and supportive framework.

In describing approaches for intervention with many types of traumatized children, Beverly James (1989) lists the following considerations for therapy: (a) exploration of emotional pain; (b) continued treatment at various developmental ages and levels; (c) active participation of caregivers; (d) direct approaches to material that may not be produced spontaneously in therapy; (e) enjoyable, positive clinical messages which attend to all of the child's damaged parts (physical, cognitive, emotional, etc.); and (f) a focus on discovering and dealing with secret dysfunctional, sexualized deviant behaviors.

In further support of dealing directly with the abuse experience, Berliner and Wheeler (1987) has written that direct confrontation, not only of the abuse itself but also of victims' negative coping responses, fear, anxiety, and sexual behavior problems, should be combined with therapeutic interventions to address specific family or child behaviors, perceptions, and functioning.

In other work with this population, Scheinberg, True, and Fraenkel (1994) have used a multimodal approach to address many of these criteria. By combining individual, group, and family therapies, they propose that specific problems revealed during treatment can be addressed in any one of the three modalities. Although in reality many facilities are unable to provide such a spectrum of separate but interrelated interventions, Scheinberg et al.'s emphasis on interpersonal work with peers and family members is shared by most other writers and practitioners.

The American Academy of Child and Adolescent Psychiatry's *Textbook of Child and Adolescent Psychiatry* (Yates, 1991), for example, suggests that family therapy may be the most effective intervention when reunification of the family is the goal of treatment. Although individual therapy is considered to be more necessary for severely disturbed or dysfunctional children, group therapy is viewed as most useful for support and restructuring soon after abuse is discovered.

For adolescents in particular, given their predominant focus on peer interactions, group therapy is often the treatment of choice. Berkowitz and Sugar (1975) list the goals of adolescent group therapy: (a) to support assistance and confrontation from peers; (b) to provide a miniature real-life situation; (c) to develop new ways of dealing with situations in human relations; (d) to stimulate new concepts of self and new models of identification; (e) to alleviate feelings of isolation; (f) to provide protection from the adult world; (g) to help maintain continued self-examination as a "bind" to therapy; (h) to allow the swings of rebellion and submission that encourage independence and identification with a group leader; and (i) to uncover relationship problems not evident in individual therapy.

Our own work (Corder, Whiteside, & Vogel, 1977) indicates that adolescents most value goals a, c, and e above. Following Yalom's research with adults, we studied the situations and conditions of group process selected as most and least curative by adolescents in various groups. Our group members most valued group experiences that offered opportunities for, in their words, "being able to say what was bothering me instead of holding it in," "learning how to express my feelings," "learning that I must take ultimate responsibility for the way I live my life," and "having other members honestly tell me what they think of me." For one member, "being in the group was, in a sense, like being in a big family, only this time, a more accepting and understanding family."

Treatment that fosters these "curative factors" of learning and belonging is clearly helpful for sexually abused children and adolescents, because it encourages the mastery exhibited by invulnerable children. For children and adolescents alike, group therapy can provide rich opportunities to further treatment goals involving coping skills, problem-solving, and interpersonal skills in addition to positive intellectualization and self-esteem.

CHAPTER 3

A Group Psychotherapy Program

HISTORY AND RATIONALE

Synthesizing the research, theories, and approaches cited in Chapters 1 and 2 with our own clinical experience with sexually abused children and adolescents, my co-workers and I (Corder & Haizlip, 1989; Corder, Haizlip, & DeBoer, 1990) have developed psychotherapy groups for preadolescent and adolescent girls over the course of the past 30 years.

Our structured approach in these groups focuses on (a) exploring cathartic, shared emotional responses to abuse, (b) teaching techniques for mastery of the abuse experience, (c) encouraging development of some of the coping skills demonstrated by "invulnerable" children, (d) discouraging vulnerability to further abuse, (e) improving intellectual understanding of the abuse experience by both child and primary caregiver, and (f) improving communication between the child and the caregiver about the experience.

We have chosen group therapy as the basic intervention because it provides interaction with peers and helps to ameliorate two typical symptoms of abuse: the child's sense of "differentness" and that of being "damaged." Using a direct, structured approach with goals similar to those of authors cited in the preceding chapters, we have been able to use available treatment time to address the abuse experience, emotional responses, and current dysfunctional behaviors in an open and direct manner. Our concern that this structured approach might not allow for enough individualized response from group members is balanced against the restraints of time. We believe that the very directness of the structured group approach mitigates feelings of shame and perceptions of the experience as too deviant to be discussed matter-of-factly.

Our groups have focused on techniques that may help children to acquire some of the coping skills possessed by the "invulnerable" children described by Rutter (1978) and others. We believe that some of these skills, although they may have developed in an intuitive fashion among "invulnerable" children, can, at least to some extent, be taught to abused children as learned coping mechanisms.

GOALS OF STRUCTURED GROUP PSYCHOTHERAPY FOR
SEXUALLY ABUSED CHILDREN AND ADOLESCENTS

General goals for these groups have been as follows:

1. *Improving cognitive and emotional mastery of the trauma* through group activities and processes such as drawing, games, and story-telling. This involves techniques for emotional catharsis, intellectual understanding of the abuse process, relaxation techniques, anger release, and improved communication skills. In addition, the motivations and treatment of abusers are investigated.
2. *Building self-esteem* through cognitive relabeling practice that uses role-playing, group chants and cheers, and game activities to teach intellectual understanding of the abuse, the abuser, and family reactions. These games and activities help remove children's feelings of rejection and "differentness." Intended to negate child victims' feelings of shame and blame, specific material includes information about the frequency of abuse in our society, the abuser's responsibility for the abuse, involuntary pleasurable responses, and using abuse to satisfy needs for closeness.
3. *Improving problem-solving skills* using original board games, structured stories, role-playing, and so forth. These techniques focus on encouraging group members' abilities to identify and deal with potentially abusive situations, acquiring basic techniques for self-protection, and learning how to seek out and approach helping adults. Children are taught how to seek support from authority figures and facilities in their environment in order to meet their needs in ways that will not endanger them for further abuse. Appropriate and nonthreatening techniques for meeting needs for closeness and intimacy are encouraged and explored.
4. *Developing or improving communications, understanding, and coping between mother or caregiver and child victim.* Through homework assignments, actual parent/caregiver participation during specific sessions, and didactic material concerning common parent concerns, group members are given skills and confidence that improve their family relationships.

In addition to providing many opportunities, through games and activities, for cathartic release, our groups teach facts and skills, including negotiation and communication skills. Our group members are given training in cognitive techniques (visualization, thought-stopping, etc.) and in relaxation and the use of biofeedback techniques. These skills, useful in many types of interventions, fit well into our model of increasing individuals' sense of control over their bodies and environments (Corder, Whiteside, & Haizlip, 1986). Strobel and Glueck (1973, p. 380) have written that this type of training is a structured form of "self-learning to incorporate the concept of individual responsibility" that places people in a "position of importance in their own prevention and treatment programs." It encourages a sense of mastery over memories and feelings engendered by the abuse experience.

Specific techniques for providing structure and some of the therapeutic games and materials we have used differ with the developmental and chronological ages of children and adolescents; however, the basic goals for all groups are the same. These techniques and materials, developed for two different age groups, are discussed more fully in Part III of this book.

PART II

FORMING A STRUCTURED PSYCHOTHERAPY GROUP FOR ABUSED CHILDREN

CHAPTER 4

Nontherapy Issues

REFERRALS

In typical cases, our clients have been referred to us after the protective services department or social service agencies have verified abuse and made adjustments in the children's environment to ensure their safety and protection. This has usually taken place over the course of 2 or 3 months, during which time the clients have likely experienced some individual and/or family therapy sessions (usually with the primary caretaker or mother).

The few children who have suffered extreme physical abuse or violent sexual coercion are not initially referred for group therapy following the determination process; they generally remain in individual therapy, sometimes for as long as a year or more, before joining a group. Because their abuse was very different from the experience of typical group members, we have felt that their feeling of "differentness" might be exacerbated rather than alleviated by the group. Nevertheless, much of the teaching material and many of the activities developed for the group can also be used in individual sessions with children who have been severely or violently abused.

SELECTION OF GROUP MEMBERS: AGE AND DEVELOPMENTAL ISSUES

We have generally chosen six to eight girls* for a group, placing them into the following age categories: ages 6 to 9, 10 to 12, and 13 to 16. It is helpful to keep ages and social/developmental skills of group members within a 3- to 4-year range. The reasons for this are fairly clear: one member who functions noticeably differently from the others often requires extra attention from group leaders, detracting from other members' participation and from the group's process. A child's deviant functioning may also elicit the group's tendency to scapegoat its lower functioning members.

---

*Although originally used in groups of girls, these materials and processes have also been successfully used in individual sessions with boys. Principles used for selecting members for girls' groups will also, we believe, govern selection in boys' groups.

Particularly in this population, the chronological age of group members should be viewed in light of their past and current experiences. Some of the girls in our groups have seemed "6 going on 18," while others were highly dependent 16-year-olds functioning at preadolescent levels. It is not unlikely that children's deviant functioning is related to their abuse experiences, and they may need to be "given permission" to behave appropriately — in other words, to stop performing as a preadolescent who is avoiding their sexuality, or as an adult child. Such performances, often ingrained in the personality traits and behavior patterns of sexual abuse victims, are sometimes best addressed by referring them, at least initially, to a group whose members are functioning at similar levels, regardless of age.

GENDER, SOCIOECONOMIC, AND FAMILY ISSUES

Clinical experience dictates that younger children in particular, who frequently experience increased anxiety and attention problems in mixed groups, be placed in same-sex groups. Due to the aforementioned lack of male referrals, this has not been an issue for us; however, feedback from Dr. Michael Rutter (personal communication, 1990), who has supervised many similar groups in England, reinforces same-sex grouping. Rutter believes that treatment groups should reflect the social interaction patterns of children at their various developmental levels and ages. Because sexual issues are generally not easily discussed in mixed adolescent and teen groups and because we have had so few male referrals, our older groups have also consisted entirely of girls.

The majority of group members have been within the average range of intellectual functioning (again, we have tried to avoid member "deviance"). It has been possible to include a fairly wide range of socioeconomic backgrounds within the groups, and even though some members have been removed from their homes, their treatment plans have included some form of family reintegration. It has been important for members to learn that family dynamics can be healthy regardless of socioeconomic or educational status. Materials dealing with aspects of family functioning are relevant to all members of the group.

Primary caretakers are involved in our group process. We believe it is necessary to request that the mother or caretaker attend several sessions, particularly those focusing on family issues. If a primary caretaker is not available, another adult who is involved in the child's case should attend and agree to help the child with group homework assignments. The involvement of caretakers is discussed more fully in Chapters 5 and 6.

ADMINISTRATIVE ISSUES

A number of issues concerning inter- and intraagency cooperation must be addressed in order to conduct psychotherapy groups for sexually abused children. As with any treatment group, the "ownership" of the group is always an issue. Lines of administration and communication should be clearly stated, and persons directly responsible for decision making should be identified to all parties. It is important to develop and follow a written procedure manual. At the very least, this manual should describe agency communication and recordkeeping procedures, chain of command, and group psychotherapy functions. The manual may also include information on confidentiality guidelines, group rules, required feedback to parents and others, and so on.

Primary or Adjunct Therapy

This issue must be considered administratively as well as clinically. If the group is considered adjunct therapy and the child or family is involved in other weekly or ongoing interventions, it is essential to establish lines of communication between therapists in order to maintain coherent treatment goals. Identifying a "primary therapist" ensures consistent strategies for treatment. In many cases, groups are conducted under the umbrella of social services functions. The legal liability for the group and administrative lines for day-to-day functioning must be established.

Whether or not the group is considered the child's primary therapy, it must be determined whether group leaders will have access to each child's chart, both before and during the group. Permission forms, confidentiality issues, and communications policies should be delineated well in advance of the first group meeting.

Confidentiality Issues

Confidentiality is especially critical in sexual abuse groups. In our groups, the facts concerning the abuse and its legal consequences usually have been determined before a child has been referred to our groups. In a few instances, however, group leaders have requested specific information regarding legal charges against the perpetrator; in our case, fortunately, the agency's therapy contract with each child and parent outlines confidentiality issues and restraints. It is always helpful to have a clear record of the expectations of the client and parent/caregiver with regard to confidentiality in order to avoid conflict.

Recordkeeping and Confidentiality

Keeping detailed notes for each child's weekly functioning can be overwhelmingly burdensome. Individual recordkeeping systems differ from agency to agency; our experience has been that it is usually acceptable to write a fairly detailed summary for each session in which children are identified by initials only, and to place a copy of that one summary in each child's chart. In some instances where confidentiality has appeared to be a more urgent issue, we have disguised initials by using one letter forward for each initial (e.g., Alice Martin, A. M., becomes B. N.).

THE PHYSICAL SETTING

Younger children will require a table, clipboard, or other slatelike individual surface for coloring and drawing. They can easily sit on a clean, carpeted floor, but it is helpful to have a collection of small chairs to use at other times. Adolescents will require an adequate supply of comfortable chairs (all alike to avoid arguing over favorite chairs). Some therapists prefer using a large conference table, especially in early sessions, but this is not a necessity in our experience. A small table is helpful for serving refreshments.

REFRESHMENTS

Most therapists agree that serving refreshments is enjoyable for the group. It possesses a symbolic function as well: The act of offering food provides children with a feeling of being nurtured and portrays the therapists as helping, caring adults (James, 1989). Sharing food is useful for teaching social skills and for empowering group members to help one another, because it is an activity that can be "taken over" by the group. Serving refreshments is one of the structured roles that we assign to our group members, as described in Part III.

Refreshments should be as simple as possible — perhaps a fruit-filled cookie or granola bar and juice or sodas. Each parent/caregiver should be asked, preferably during pregroup orientation, if there are particular foods his or her child cannot eat.

LENGTH OF SESSIONS

Most younger children have difficulty giving their attention to the group for more than an hour, which should probably be the time limit for sessions. Teens may be able to profit from as long as an hour and one-half, but extending the group longer than this is usually counterproductive. Many agencies with which we have worked have transportation limitations which require an hour for all groups. The structured groups described in Part III can be effective within that time frame.

CHAPTER 5

Clinical Issues: Pregroup Orientation

PREGROUP MEETINGS

It has not always been possible for us to meet individually with all members and their caregivers before the beginning of the group, although this is very helpful. When possible, the pregroup individual meetings focus on explaining the purpose of the group, demonstrating some of the materials and procedures we will use, and developing a contract with child and caregiver, which they and the therapist will sign. (See contracts on pages 20-23.)

We have found that the actual signing of the contract is taken quite seriously by young children as well as adolescents. The ceremonial signing concretizes the goals of the group and emphasizes the importance of group members' expectations.

PRETESTING

The administration of pretest questionnaires is an important aspect of preparing members, caretakers, and therapists for the group. Pretesting and posttesting are covered in more detail in Chapter 8; however, pretesting is mentioned here because it is invaluable for assessing the needs of individual group members and because it is a task that should be completed before the onset of the group. Because it is sometimes difficult, administratively, to use treatment time for what some agencies have termed "research," therapists should consider how and when pretesting will be administered. (In one instance, while we were preparing for a group for sexually abused girls, our pretesting was labeled as research. Transportation services, which were to be utilized for treatment time only, were denied.) When pregroup orientation meetings are not possible, we have utilized time during the first group session to administer pretests. This is an important (and time-consuming) consideration for younger children, in particular, because the questions must be read aloud to them. Parents are given their own questionnaire, which details the child's behavior at home, at some point before the first group meeting. (For information about specific measures and questionnaire items, please see Chapter 8.)

THE THERAPY CONTRACT

A sample of the structured group therapy contract is included on pages 20-21. A reproducible version of that contract for use in actual structured groups appears on pages 22-23. Some other examples of therapy contracts can be found in Corder (1987).

Instructions for Using the Contract

The contract on pages 22-23 can be photocopied directly from this book for use with your clients. Where "he/she" is indicated, simply cross out or circle to indicate the child's gender. You may also cross out inapplicable activities (such as coloring books for teenagers).

QUESTIONS COMMONLY ASKED BY PARENTS AND CAREGIVERS

Before a group commences, parents/caretakers (usually mothers) have often expressed concerns or asked questions about the group. To clarify both their questions and the nature of our responses, as many as possible have been included here.

Question: Won't talking about all this just make my child more nervous about the abuse?

Answer: A lot of research and clinical work has indicated that the opposite happens. Children who bottle up their feelings and aren't able to discuss them usually have more symptoms, either now or later in life. We will be talking about them in a safe way without making anyone say more than they want to say. This will involve using games, art, and some other techniques that encourage group members to feel comfortable and not put them "on the spot."

Question: Is this a bad thing to be talking so much about sex with little children? Could it make their problem worse?

Answer: They have already been exposed to some kind of sex and are probably confused and worried about it. We will not be talking about things they have not already had some type of experience with. What we will be doing is helping them deal emotionally and intellectually with their feelings about these experiences. All the research and clinical work we know about shows that they need to understand about sexual abuse so they can handle their feelings and learn to emotionally handle what has happened to them.

Question: What if some of the other girls have had really serious sexual abuse which is much worse than my child's? Will this make her more frightened or worry more about sex when the other girls talk about their experiences?

Answer: First, none of the girls in this group has been violently physically abused. But the seriousness of sexual abuse is also measured by the seriousness of the child's emotional reactions to it. What we know is this: It is very helpful to girls to hear and understand that they are not the only ones this has happened to. Feeling very "different" is one of the most negative feelings they have to deal with. Being with other girls who have experienced abuse is very important in helping them to understand how many girls in our country have experienced abuse — about one in five, according to some statistics.

Question: I have heard that some girls blame their mothers/caretakers for the abuse their fathers/boyfriends* committed. Will the group let my daughter blame me?

---

*Although most references in this book focus on male abusers, abuse is not a gender-specific phenomenon. There are also women who abuse and appropriate corrections for the abuser's gender should be made when working with abused children and adolescents.

Answer: We work a lot on understanding why it is hard for mothers/caretakers to understand about the abuse. In fact, we try to help girls and their mothers/caretakers understand each other's feelings about why the abuse could happen. You will be coming to some of the sessions while we are doing this. You'll hear how we try to help both of you understand.

Question: Is the group just going to make her hate my husband (boyfriend) more? Because after he has treatment, maybe we will be back together someday. Will she expect me to hate him completely? Because I still have some love for him.

Answer: One of the things the group works on is understanding why people abuse children. This sometimes helps victims to deal with their feelings. We also work on understanding that most people, both parents and children, may have conflicting feelings toward abusers: love for their good qualities and hate for their abuse. But we will have to work on how your child must try to keep herself safe from any further abuse. We expect that you will work on this also.

Question: I was sexually abused as a child, but I never told my daughter this. Do you think I should tell her before she is in the group?

Answer: That will be up to you. Some mothers/caretakers have talked about this during the group session when we talked about some of the things that are sometimes present in homes where abuse takes place. We generally feel that this is a helpful thing to share, because you can also share your feelings and worries about the experience. However, it is very difficult for most people to share these things, and you might want to wait until we are talking about them in the group, where you will have our help and the support of the other mothers/caretakers, many of whom have also been abused in the past.

Question: The whole family had to give up a lot when they removed (husband, boyfriend) from the home. You'd think she would appreciate this and try to be more of a help to me, instead of being even more disrespectful. Will this group just teach her more about feeling angry with me and make her even harder to get along with?

Answer: Girls are often angry with their mothers or caretakers because they think you should have known what was going on. This is one of the reasons they act up at home after the abuse has been discovered. One of the things we work on in the group is understanding how hard it is for parents/caretakers to accept and believe facts about the abuse. You will attend some of the sessions about this. Two of our goals are (a) to understand why believing the abuse is difficult and (b) to learn to solve problems and make compromises at home so that the whole family can get on with their lives.

SAMPLE CONTRACT

FOR GROUP THERAPY FOR
SEXUALLY ABUSED CHILDREN AND ADOLESCENTS

We, ____*(the group member)*____, ____*(parent or caretaker)*____, and ___*(group therapist)*___ agree that _____*(the group member)*_____ will attend _*(number)*_ group sessions of a group for sexually abused children/adolescents at _____*(facility)*_____, which will meet each _____*(day)*_____ at _____*(time)*_____, from _____*(day and month)*_____ to _____*(day, month, and year)*_____. Transportation to and from the group will be arranged by _____*(usually the facility)*_____. Cost for the group will be handled by _____*(usually the facility)*_____.

Goals and Purpose of This Group

The purpose of this group will be to help ____*(the group member)*____ and ___*(parent or caretaker)*___ understand:

1. The facts about what causes abuse to happen,
2. That the abuse is not your fault,
3. That your feelings about the abuse are natural,
4. That many, many other children have also been abused and you are not the only one, and
5. That it is very difficult for most families to understand about the abuse right away, but they usually are finally able to understand.

You will also learn:

6. That you can still feel good about yourself, and how to do this,
7. That you can keep yourself safe and how to do this,
8. Who you can go to for help in keeping yourself safe and how to ask for any help you need,
9. How to handle your feelings about the abuse by learning how to talk about it and express your feelings, and
10. How to handle the nervous feelings you still have by learning how to relax and how to keep safe.

What Is Expected from ____*(the group member)*____ and ___*(parent or caretaker)*___ :

____*(The group member)*____ is expected to be at the group on time each session. In the group, you must give everyone a time to talk without interrupting each other, pay attention to the things we are doing, and try to work on each exercise in the group. Everything that is said in the group is between the members and therapists, although you will be encouraged to share some things about the group with ____*(parent or caretaker)*____. The only time something would be told to _*(parent or caretaker)*_ or others is if you say you are doing something that is harmful to yourself or other people (like taking drugs or trying to hurt yourself or someone else, or if someone is still trying to abuse you).

(Parent or Caretaker) is asked to come periodically every _(number)_ sessions, and it is important that you attend. You are also asked to help _(the group member)_ with some simple "homework" at home before the next session. You are asked to give your child "permission" to say whatever he/she likes in the group and to talk openly about the abuse.

What We Will Be Doing in the Group

We will be learning and talking about all these things in some fun ways. There will be coloring books, drawing, board games, acting-out "plays," and sometimes just talking with each other.

(OPTIONAL SECTION, DEPENDENT UPON THE AGE OF CHILD)

Personal Goals: In the group, one of the main things I would like to work on:

My bad feelings and temper .

SIGNATURES: We understand about the purposes of the group and agree to attend and work on the things in this contract.

SIGNED:

Mrs. Molly Doe (Parent/Caretaker) Date: 5/15/00

Jane Doe (Group Member) Date: 5/15/00

Mary Smith (Therapist) Date: 5/15/00

CONTRACT

FOR GROUP THERAPY FOR
SEXUALLY ABUSED CHILDREN AND ADOLESCENTS

We, _____, _____, and _____

agree that _____ will attend _____ group sessions of a group for

sexually abused children/adolescents at _____, which will

meet each _____ at _____,

from _____ to _____.

Transportation to and from the group will be arranged by _____.

Cost for the group will be handled by _____.

Goals and Purpose of This Group

The purpose of this group will be to help _____ and _____ understand:

1. The facts about what causes abuse to happen,
2. That the abuse is not your fault,
3. That your feelings about the abuse are natural,
4. That many, many other children have also been abused and you are not the only one, and
5. That it is very difficult for most families to understand about the abuse right away, but they usually are finally able to understand.

You will also learn:

6. That you can still feel good about yourself, and how to do this,
7. That you can keep yourself safe and how to do this,
8. Who you can go to for help in keeping yourself safe and how to ask for any help you need,
9. How to handle your feelings about the abuse by learning how to talk about it and express your feelings, and
10. How to handle the nervous feelings you still have by learning how to relax and how to keep safe.

What Is Expected from _____ and _____:

_____ is expected to be at the group on time each session. In the group, you must give everyone a time to talk without interrupting each other, pay attention to the things we are doing, and try to work on each exercise in the group. Everything that is said in the group is between the members and therapists, although you will be encouraged to share some things about the group with _____. The only time something would be told to _____ or others is if you say you are doing something that is harmful to yourself or other people (like taking drugs or trying to hurt yourself or someone else, or if someone is still trying to abuse you).

_____ is asked to come periodically every _____ sessions, and it is important that you attend. You are also asked to help _____ with some simple "homework" at home before the next session. You are asked to give your child "permission" to say whatever he/she likes in the group and to talk openly about the abuse.

What We Will Be Doing in the Group

We will be learning and talking about all these things in some fun ways. There will be coloring books, drawing, board games, acting-out "plays," and sometimes just talking with each other.

(OPTIONAL SECTION, DEPENDENT UPON THE AGE OF CHILD)

Personal Goals: In the group, one of the main things I would like to work on:

_____

_____.

SIGNATURES: We understand about the purposes of the group and agree to attend and work on the things in this contract.

SIGNED:

_____ (Parent/Caretaker)   Date:_____

_____ (Group Member)   Date: _____

_____ (Therapist)   Date: _____

CHAPTER 6

Clinical Issues: Including Parents and Caretakers in Groups

WHY AND HOW WE INCLUDE PARENTS/CARETAKERS*

Beverly James (1989), internationally known for her work with traumatized children, has emphasized the importance of including parents in their child's treatment. When possible, parents/caretakers should have the opportunity to be involved with other parents whose children have experienced trauma, to explore their feelings, reactions, and plans for the future. Despite our emphasis on the importance of separate parents' groups, in most instances in our practice such groups have not been feasible, for reasons either financial, administrative, or both.

Our response has been to include parents in a certain number of group sessions with their children. Although we do not see this as ideal, it meets the requirements for what James (1989, p. 10) has described as "minimum" to "medium" parental involvement. Her criteria for "maximum" parental involvement, in which parents work directly with the therapist to plan and lead individual sessions and to involve other family members, are rarely possible in time-limited treatment modalities. In our groups, parental participation occurs via four methods: the parent (a) completes a behavioral assessment of the child, (b) attends some of the sessions, (c) assists with weekly homework, and (d) receives frequent telephone calls from therapists for updates on home and school behavior.

The importance of parents' involvement with their children's treatment cannot be overemphasized. Rutter (personal communication, 1995), has noted that the child will be returned to the parent after therapy, and that without some form of parent training and intervention, continued work toward treatment goals is unlikely to occur. In addition, our legal advisors have stressed the importance of parents' understanding our treatment goals and techniques. Without this understanding and permission, confusion and legal entanglements are possible.

FREQUENT PARENTS' ISSUES

Initial issues to be settled with parents during pregroup orientation and the contract-signing are discussed in the previous chapter's Question/Answer section. There are other therapeutic issues likely

---

*The terms *parent, mother, father, caretaker,* and *caregiver* are used interchangeably in this book to refer to the child's or adolescent's parents and other responsible caregivers.

to surface, however, for which therapists should be prepared. These include (a) parent/caretaker guilt at not having recognized the abuse and intervened to protect the child; (b) the parent's ambivalent feelings and needs for keeping the abuser within the environment; (c) renewed anxieties of parents who have been abused themselves (this has been common in our groups; approximately one-fifth, or 20%, of parents/caretakers have disclosed their own previous abuse); (d) the parent's willingness and ability to learn how to help the child express her feelings and develop self-esteem, mastery, and a sense of safety; and (e) the parent's willingness and ability to deal with daily parent-child conflicts, some of which may be related to how the abuse was initially handled in the home.

STRUCTURING PARENTS' ATTENDANCE

Once these issues are faced, therapists will decide which sessions the parents should attend and specify the dates with both children and parents/caretakers. We have found it more productive to plan for parents' structured participation than to allow them to attend on a random or constant basis as observers. Many parents of abused children have serious concerns about entrusting their children to strangers, even in an approved setting; one possible solution to this concern is a room with one-way mirrors (without sound systems, to protect confidentiality) so that parents can observe.

Because some parents are unable to leave work on a regular basis, the therapist must also designate a surrogate (i.e., social worker, case manager, or significant adult in a child's life) to attend during the sessions in which adults will be present when a particular child's parent cannot be.

In our groups, adult participation depends on the ages of the group members. In younger children's groups (ages 6-9 and 10-12), the parent's participation is somewhat passive: the parent attends sessions, helps the child with drawing, games, and role-play; and observes role-modeling by the therapist. After the initial session, we ask that parents attend every other group therapy session.

In adolescent and teen groups (ages 13-16), parents usually attend every third session. One of the tasks of adolescence is to separate from parents, and parents in these groups are generally more active and verbal than those in the younger children's groups.

SUPPORT FOR PARENTS

As noted, a separate support group to address specific parenting issues and to prepare parents for participation in their children's groups would be most helpful; however, we have seldom been able to implement these groups. Through group homework assignments and telephone conversations, we have usually been able to provide feedback and support; moreover, parents' presence in their children's groups is valuable to both parties. A mother's "permission" for her daughter to express angry, conflicted feelings, and her reassurance to her that she is "normal" and loved, are very important functions of the group. By the same token, even though parents may have learned from therapists or peers that their own guilt and conflicted feelings are normal, it is a powerful experience to understand and be understood, to affirm and be affirmed, by other parents in the presence of their children.

In Part III of this book, which outlines specific group session formats, the role of parents/caretakers in every second or third group session is more fully discussed. I wish to emphasize that our "formula" for parent involvement is what we have found works best within the limitations of the treatment facilities, parent transportation and attendance problems, and other issues in the facilities where we have held groups. Readers will encounter other limitations and opportunities and may adapt this format accordingly.

CHAPTER 7

Clinical Issues: Decisions Therapists Must Make Before Initiating the Group

NECESSARY PERSONAL SKILLS

James and Nasjleti (1994) list the following personal qualities necessary for therapists treating sexually abused children: an ability to deal comfortably with expressions of pain, helplessness, and grief; ease in dealing with personal sexuality and sexual issues discussed in groups; open, honest communication skills; ability to assume control when necessary; a good sense of humor; and ability to demonstrate an open, emotionally appropriate relationship with a co-therapist which is not sexualized.

LEVELS OF INTIMACY AND DISCLOSURE

Particularly in groups of this nature, co-therapists need to discuss in advance the level of intimacy at which they will reveal their own personal experiences in response to questions. Children may ask therapists about themselves and their sexuality, and although curious, they are more typically asking, "Are you so different from me that you will think I am bad?" There are three questions to which every group member wants and deserves answers; these are:

- What is "normal" for sexual experiences?
- Are you really capable of understanding my experiences?
- Can you accept what has happened to me and still like and respect me?

Although each therapist must be able to respond personally and comfortably, he or she should keep these questions in mind. Children do not need or even want to know the details of the therapist's life; they are more interested in understanding what is "normal." Therapists should be able to help their group members understand "normal." They must be aware that children are really asking for reassurance of their self-worth.

Here is an example of how this is accomplished: In a young group conducted by the author and a male co-therapist, one child asked the male co-therapist, "Do you ever have sex with your little girl? Do all daddies have sex with their little girls?" His response: "No. All daddies do not have sex with their little girls, and I do not. I have love feelings for my little girl and love feelings for my wife. They are two different things. The love feelings I have for my wife have to do with love that includes grown-up sex, but the love feelings toward my little girl do not include sex. Some men are mixed up in their heads about love feelings and who to show them to. This is like a kind of sickness, or sometimes they just don't care enough about anybody to sort them out. These are the kind of daddies that have sex with their little girls. I think you may be asking me if your daddy is just like everybody else's daddy. He is not, although this happens to many young girls. But it is his fault that it happened. He should know better, or try to work out his love feelings so that he would know what was the right way to show love feelings to you."

In another case, a child asked the (female) therapist when she first had sex. Her reply was: "I think you may really be asking me if anybody else has sex at your age. Most people have sex when they and the person they have sex with are old enough to understand about real love and responsibility and taking care of each other. But many people are sexually abused by another person when they are really too young to understand or make a real choice about it. Some little babies are even abused. A lot of people who study these things say that one out of every five girls in this country have sexual things happen to them which are abuse. That means they were not ready, or maybe not old enough, for sex and the abuser was doing it for his (her) pleasure without caring what was best or right for you. So you are not alone in what happened to you. And in this group we are going to learn what abuse is, that it happens to lots and lots of people, that it was not your fault, and how to keep it from happening again. We will even talk about what is the right time and way for people to show their real true, loving feelings toward each other."

Specific replies might be different from the preceding examples, but they should resonate with phrases and words that affirm to the child, "You are not alone. You are a good person. The abuse is not your fault. You will be able to have a good life, and we are here to help you."

CRITICAL GROUP ISSUES AND POTENTIAL PROBLEMS

In addition to issues of intimacy, before a group's first meeting its co-therapists should discuss plans for handling group process, problems, and crises. A single group leader should also make plans and decisions concerning these issues. Anxiety levels can escalate quickly, particularly in adolescent groups, and advance planning helps immensely during situations that are potentially destructive or counterproductive.

ASK YOURSELF BEFORE YOU BEGIN

Below are some challenges concerning policy and group process. Group therapists should reach decisions and agreement about each issue before the first group meets. Advice on some of them is provided, albeit sometimes indirectly, elsewhere in this book; however, most are matters of personal and professional judgment requiring your decisive forethought and collaboration with your co-therapist.

✓ How will you as co-therapists "even up" your input in groups? Who will do what (introduce topics, summarize session, etc.) in group?

✓ What will you do if a child (teen) becomes more graphic or explicit in explaining situations or incidents than you think appropriate for the group?

- ✓ How will you handle any scapegoating which can take place when one member's responses and behavior appears deviant from the others'?
- ✓ Beyond what is part of the planned session structure, how much input from parents/caretakers will you allow?
- ✓ How will you handle inappropriate input from parents/caretakers?
- ✓ How will you handle a child (teen) who seems withdrawn and responds little to the structured activities of the session?
- ✓ If group members (either parents/caretakers or children) are involved in other types of therapy, how should this be integrated with the group?
- ✓ How will you deal with a group member who suddenly becomes very upset, cries, or dashes from the room?
- ✓ How will you deal with material that indicates that inappropriate sexual activity may still be going on in the child's (teen's) home or environment?
- ✓ How will you deal with extremely negative or harsh comments from a group member made to either another group member or the therapists?
- ✓ How will you handle inappropriate or very negative interactions between parent/caretaker and child in the session?
- ✓ If a member shows or threatens physical aggression in the group, how will you handle it?
- ✓ When a group member appears to be using all the group's time without allowing others to share, how will you handle the situation?
- ✓ How will you know when the group's anxiety level has risen to unproductive levels, and what will you do about it?
- ✓ How will you keep records about the group process?
- ✓ Will your group be one that is strictly "closed," or will you allow members to join once the group has begun?
- ✓ Will you have access to supervision or collaborative assistance for discussion of persistent problems?
- ✓ What type of follow-up will you develop for the group?
- ✓ To whom and where can members who appear to need much more intervention be referred?
- ✓ What confidentiality measures will you take in recordkeeping or feedback to staff and/or parents/caretakers?
- ✓ What are your general goals with this group, and how will you measure your progress?
- ✓ What are the specific goals for each structured session, and how can you measure your effectiveness?
- ✓ How will you handle physical expressions of affection in the group which you do not feel are appropriate (either between members or toward therapists)?
- ✓ How will you decide that a group member is simply not profiting from the group and is a destructive factor? What will you do about it?

Program Evaluation:
Pre- and Posttesting Group Members

MEASURING FOR CLINICAL EFFECTIVENESS

Assessment of treatment is crucial for anyone who wants to improve his or her ability to provide critical interventions for children. Therapists interested in their clinical effectiveness and growth must not overlook pretesting and follow-up evaluation, which represent the only objective means for anticipating individual needs, measuring individual progress, and determining the group's efficacy.

There are a number of standardized behavioral assessment measures that can be useful for this purpose. One tool for looking at a child or adolescent's general behavior patterns is the *Devereux Scale of Psychopathology* (Naglieri, LeBuffe, & Pfeiffer, 1992), which is available in forms for ages 5 to 12 and 13 to 18. This is a scale of 110 items which attempts to identify children and adolescents who are at risk for emotional or behavior disorders. Another measure, the *Connors Rating Scales* (Connors, 1978), is completed by a parent or teacher of children ages 3 to 17.

Questionnaires for children to complete themselves are also extremely useful. The *Children's Personality Questionnaire* (Porter & Cattell, 1984) for ages 8 through 15, and the *Children's Depression Inventory* (Kovacks, 1992) for ages 7 to 17, specify first grade reading level abilities. Another assessment device, the *Revised Children's Manifest Anxiety Scale* (Gillis, Reynolds, & Richmond, 1993), is listed as appropriate for ages 5 to 12.

Unfortunately, these tests are not specifically geared toward measuring the effects of trauma, and they may not show strong changes in general behavior after a treatment program. For this reason we have developed the Corder Pre- and Posttreatment Scales, which may be used separately or in conjunction with some of the commercially available measures mentioned previously.

The Corder scales are useful not only as pre- and postgroup measures of beliefs and behaviors, but also as pregroup activities, because they help to prepare group members and their caregivers for some of the didactic material presented in the groups. Not intended as scientific measurements, their primary purpose is for the group therapist's edification and review.

THE CORDER PRE- AND POSTTREATMENT SCALES

There are two scales, one for adult caregivers and one for group members. The first, a questionnaire administered to parents and caregivers, addresses the frequency of symptom occurrence, asking caregivers to estimate how often they observe certain behaviors typical of sexually abused or invulnerable children. This questionnaire has two versions, one for children ages 6 to 9 and another for those 10 and older. The second version contains additional questions appropriate to the developmental level of that population.

The group members' scale, on the other hand, seeks to determine group members' attitudes, beliefs, and feelings (as opposed to behaviors) about the abuse they experienced. This scale is the same for both younger and older children, with the exception that choices on the answer sheet for 6- to 9-year-olds are "true," "not true," and "not sure," and choices for older members are "true," "sort of true," "false," and "sort of false." The group members' scale contains some factual items of an impersonal nature (e.g., "It is the child's own fault that he or she gets sexually abused") and others more personally directed ("People can look at you and know that you have probably been sexually abused").

As part of the group members' scale, The "Worry List," which helps to chart the concerns of adolescents and teens, can be administered to older groups. The "Worry List" serves to reassure group members that their concerns may be shared by others who have suffered abuse. It is particularly helpful as a posttest, because it provides a view of progress to both members and group leaders. All three scales, The "Worry List," and response sheets for both age groups are included at the end of this chapter (see pp. 34-41).

ALTERNATIVES FOR ADMINISTERING THE SCALES

Because we have often been faced with transportation, time, or agency constraints, we have sometimes administered the parent/caregiver scale over the telephone. This is particularly useful for obtaining anecdotal information not necessarily prompted by the written questionnaire. Pregroup telephone contact also sets the stage for our postgroup follow-up interviews (see below).

We have also used parts of the first and last group meetings to administer the group members' scales. This is particularly useful when members' reading abilities are unknown or disparate; group leaders read the items aloud while members circle their responses on their answer sheets. An additional advantage of full-group administration of this scale is that it can serve to introduce topics for discussion and to alleviate members' feelings of "differentness."

FOLLOW-UP QUESTIONNAIRES AND INTERVIEWS

Perhaps because of too-subtle language or because our scales are designed to collect information rather than to measure change, not every group exhibits radical differences between pre- and posttest results. For this and other reasons, we also contact mothers or designated caregivers 2 weeks, 3 months, and 1 year following the last group session. We ask each for a brief verbal report on his or her child's behavior and adjustment. Typical phone interview questions include:

1. What do you think _____ got out of being in the group?
2. What do you feel you got out of coming to visit the group?
3. What changes do you think you have seen in _____'s behavior since being in the group?
4. Do you think that she/he seems less worried or shows fewer concerns about sexual abuse after she/he has been in the group, or is this about the same? If these things did change, how did they seem to be different?

5. Have you continued to see any behaviors that you feel were somehow connected to the abuse? Please tell me about them.
6. What would you have liked us to include in the group that you did not see handled or discussed?

Most parents have reported positive changes. Anecdotal and follow-up information received over time from parents, teachers, and others have made us confident that this form of group therapy has a positive effect on the behavior and perceptions of children who have been involved, although children do vary in their responses to the type of materials and structure we have employed.

The follow-up interview can also serve as a reminder and reinforcement of what was learned in the group: negotiation skills or relaxation techniques, for example.

One frequent parent/caretaker suggestion involves the request for collateral or supplemental parent/caretaker groups. We agree strongly that this multimodal approach would be preferred, but have seldom been able to secure the staffing and resources for such groups.

Instructions for Using Corder Pre- and Posttreatment Scales

The caregivers' and children's versions of the scales are on the next pages. Please note that there are two versions of the parents'/caretakers' scale, one for those with younger children (PC = parents/caretakers of children) and one for those with adolescents and teens (PT = parents/caretakers of teens). The group members' scale (GM = group members) is the same for all ages; however, the answer sheet is different. The additional "Worry List" is included for adolescents and teens and can be administered to groups whose members are competent readers.

CORDER PRE- AND POSTTREATMENT SCALE – PC

FOR PARENTS AND CARETAKERS OF CHILDREN AGES 6 TO 9

PLEASE WRITE IN THE BLANK BEFORE EACH DESCRIPTION THE NUMBER WHICH SHOWS HOW OFTEN YOUR CHILD EXHIBITS THIS BEHAVIOR:

```
1 = occurs daily
2 = occurs several times a week
3 = occurs about once a week
4 = occurs about once a month
5 = hardly ever occurs
6 = never occurs
```

_____ 1. Bursts into tears for little or no reason.

_____ 2. Seems generally upset over small things for no reason.

_____ 3. Seems and looks depressed and sad.

_____ 4. Has sleep problems (problems getting to sleep, waking up, walking in sleep).

_____ 5. Seems unusually irritable and "touchy."

_____ 6. Argues with parents over small things.

_____ 7. Says negative things about herself or himself.

_____ 8. Has discipline problems at school.

_____ 9. Does not do work at school, doesn't do homework.

_____ 10. Does not pay attention in school.

_____ 11. Gets into difficulties with others in neighborhood.

_____ 12. Shows inappropriate sexual behavior. (Describe)_____
_____

_____ 13. Shows unusual interest in her/his body or others' bodies. (Describe)_____
_____

_____ 14. Does not keep herself or himself clean or groomed.

_____ 15. Shows changes in eating habits. (Describe)_____
_____

_____ 16. Seems afraid of any stranger or others she or he does not know well.

_____ 17. Seems afraid to be left alone, or have you leave her or him.

_____ 18. Masturbates or touches herself or himself inappropriately.

_____ 19. Makes incorrect statements about the abuse and/or its cause (it was all my fault, it never happened, people can tell it happened by looking at me, etc.).

_____ 20. Is able to follow rules in home and at school.

_____ 21. Gets good notes from teacher.

_____ 22. Talks about her or his feelings with you (about everyday things or conflicts).

_____ 23. Talks about the abuse with you.

_____ 24. Shows some signs of pride in herself or himself. (Describe)_____
_____

_____ 25. Shows no particular problems with siblings or others in the neighborhood.

_____ 26. Seems relaxed and able to enjoy activities and play.

_____ 27. Is able to work though some problems or find solutions to some everyday problems herself or himself or with your help.

_____ 28. Makes some statements that show she or he has an understanding of at least some aspects of abuse (what happened was not my fault, people who abuse children have big problems, lots of people get abused, not just me, etc.).

Chapter 8 - Program Evaluation: Pre- and Posttesting Group Members

CORDER PRE- AND POSTTREATMENT SCALE – PT

FOR PARENTS AND CARETAKERS OF CHILDREN AGES 10 AND OLDER

PLEASE WRITE IN THE BLANK BEFORE EACH DESCRIPTION THE NUMBER WHICH SHOWS
HOW OFTEN YOUR CHILD EXHIBITS THIS BEHAVIOR:

```
1 = occurs daily
2 = occurs several times a week
3 = occurs about once a week
4 = occurs about once a month
5 = hardly ever occurs
6 = never occurs
```

_____ 1. Bursts into tears for little or no reason.

_____ 2. Seems generally upset over small things for no reason.

_____ 3. Seems and looks depressed and sad.

_____ 4. Has sleep problems (problems getting to sleep, waking up, walking in sleep).

_____ 5. Eating problems:
   ❑ (eats excessively)
   ❑ (eats very little)

_____ 6. Unusually irritable or "touchy."

_____ 7. Says negative things about herself or himself.

_____ 8. Has discipline problems at home.

_____ 9. Argues with you over small things.

_____ 10. Does not do chores or fulfill small family "jobs."

_____ 11. Has discipline problems at school.

_____ 12. Does not pay attention in school.

_____ 13. Does not do classwork or homework.

_____ 14. Gets into difficulties in the neighborhood. (Describe)_____

_____

_____ 15. Ignores body and clothing and appears unkempt or dirty.

_____ 16. Shows excessive concern about neatness and cleanliness.

_____ 17. Shows unusual interest about her or his own body and other people's bodies. (Describe)_____

_____

_____ 18. Seems frightened of being alone.

_____ 19. Masturbates or touches herself or himself inappropriately.

_____ 20. Dresses in an unusual, provocative, or "sexy" manner.

_____ 21. Tries to keep body completely covered at all times, wearing loose-fitting or very concealing clothing.

_____ 22. Shows unusual amount of touching, rubbing, or wanting contact with other peoples' bodies.

_____ 23. Is known or suspected to be acting out sexually (having intercourse with one or more people).

_____ 24. Openly invites sexual remarks or overtures from others by behavior, clothing, or display of body.

_____ 25. Seems frightened of any body contact or discussion of sexual behavior.

_____ 26. Seems to take many physical and/or sexual risks by engaging in dangerous activities, having unprotected sex, and going off with strangers.

_____ 27. Talks over her or his feelings with you.

_____ 28. Talks about the abuse with you or others.

_____ 29. Seems able to talk out and solve problems that occur at home.

```
1 = occurs daily
2 = occurs several times a week
3 = occurs about once a week
4 = occurs about once a month
5 = hardly ever occurs
6 = never occurs
```

_____ 30. Makes statements indicating she or he feels guilt or has negative concerns about the sexual abuse experience.

_____ 31. Makes some statements that show she or he has some understanding of some aspects of sexual abuse (i.e., the abuse was not my fault, people who abuse kids have big problems themselves, lots of people get abused, not just me).

_____ 32. Seems to have some appropriate, positive friendships with peers of the same sex.

_____ 33. Seems to have some appropriate, positive friendships with peers of the opposite sex.

_____ 34. Has some positive outlets and activities outside the home.

CORDER GROUP MEMBER PRE- AND POSTTEST – GM

FOR CHILDREN AGES 6 TO 9, OFTEN READ ALOUD

FOR EACH OF THE FOLLOWING STATEMENTS, CIRCLE ON YOUR ANSWER SHEET WHETHER YOU THINK IT IS TRUE, NOT TRUE, OR YOU ARE NOT SURE.

FOR ADOLESCENTS AND TEENS AGES 10 AND OLDER

FOR EACH OF THE FOLLOWING STATEMENTS, CIRCLE ON YOUR ANSWER SHEET WHETHER YOU THINK IT IS TRUE, SORT OF TRUE, FALSE, OR SORT OF FALSE.

1. It is the child's own fault that she or he gets sexually abused.
2. The reason children get sexually abused is because they act too sexy and that makes people want to have sex with them.
3. The main reason children don't tell about being abused is because secretly they like the sex.
4. Children get sexually abused because they are more sexy than others their age.
5. Children's mothers (caretakers) should blame the child for going along with the sexual abuse.
6. It is the mother's (caretaker's) fault that a child gets sexually abused because she or he should have known about it.
7. People can look at you and know that you have probably been sexually abused.
8. You will never be the same as other people, because you have been sexually abused.
9. When you are older or grown up, your (boyfriends, girlfriends) and (husbands, wives) will not like you as much as someone who has not been sexually abused.
10. It would be better if the child never told anyone about the abuse.
11. If a child keeps telling people about the abuse, finally somebody will help make sure the abuse is stopped.
12. It is the abuser's fault when a child is abused. Something is wrong with someone who would do this to a child.
13. There are some things a person can learn to do to keep sexual abuse from happening to her or him.
14. It is all right to feel two ways about the person who abused you (like them in some ways, and hate them in some ways).
15. I feel good about myself most of the time.
16. My life is going to get better.
17. I am going to be safe from sexual abuse.
18. I have my own rules about sexual things, and what is right and what is wrong for me.
19. I feel good about my body.
20. I think my mother (caretaker) really understands about what happened with the abuse.
21. I think my mother (caretaker) does not blame me for the abuse.
22. I think my family really understands about the abuse and does not blame me for it.
23. About one out of every five children in this country will have to work through being sexually abused. I am not the only one.
24. I will learn how to handle my feelings about sexual abuse, and I will be okay.
25. Nobody has to put up with sexual abuse, and there are ways to get people to help you stop it.

ANSWER SHEET FOR
CORDER GROUP MEMBER PRE- AND POSTTEST
(For Ages 6 to 9)

For each statement which is read aloud, circle the answer you think is right. Decide if you think it is TRUE, NOT TRUE, or if you are NOT SURE. TRUE means you agree with the sentence. NOT TRUE means you don't agree. NOT SURE means you aren't sure. Make sure you are on the right number of the statement before you circle your answer.

1.	TRUE	NOT TRUE	NOT SURE
2.	TRUE	NOT TRUE	NOT SURE
3.	TRUE	NOT TRUE	NOT SURE
4.	TRUE	NOT TRUE	NOT SURE
5.	TRUE	NOT TRUE	NOT SURE
6.	TRUE	NOT TRUE	NOT SURE
7.	TRUE	NOT TRUE	NOT SURE
8.	TRUE	NOT TRUE	NOT SURE
9.	TRUE	NOT TRUE	NOT SURE
10.	TRUE	NOT TRUE	NOT SURE
11.	TRUE	NOT TRUE	NOT SURE
12.	TRUE	NOT TRUE	NOT SURE
13.	TRUE	NOT TRUE	NOT SURE
14.	TRUE	NOT TRUE	NOT SURE
15.	TRUE	NOT TRUE	NOT SURE
16.	TRUE	NOT TRUE	NOT SURE
17.	TRUE	NOT TRUE	NOT SURE
18.	TRUE	NOT TRUE	NOT SURE
19.	TRUE	NOT TRUE	NOT SURE
20.	TRUE	NOT TRUE	NOT SURE
21.	TRUE	NOT TRUE	NOT SURE
22.	TRUE	NOT TRUE	NOT SURE
23.	TRUE	NOT TRUE	NOT SURE
24.	TRUE	NOT TRUE	NOT SURE
25.	TRUE	NOT TRUE	NOT SURE

ANSWER SHEET FOR
CORDER GROUP MEMBER PRE- AND POSTTEST
(For Ages 10 and Older)

For each statement, circle the answer you think is right. Decide if you think it is TRUE, SORT OF TRUE, FALSE, or SORT OF FALSE. TRUE means you agree with the sentence. SORT OF TRUE means that you think some things about it are true, but you do not agree completely. FALSE means you do not think the sentence is true, and you disagree with it. SORT OF FALSE means you think some things about the sentence are not true, and you do not completely disagree with it. Make sure you are on the right number of the statement before you circle your answer.

1.	TRUE	SORT OF TRUE	FALSE	SORT OF FALSE
2.	TRUE	SORT OF TRUE	FALSE	SORT OF FALSE
3.	TRUE	SORT OF TRUE	FALSE	SORT OF FALSE
4.	TRUE	SORT OF TRUE	FALSE	SORT OF FALSE
5.	TRUE	SORT OF TRUE	FALSE	SORT OF FALSE
6.	TRUE	SORT OF TRUE	FALSE	SORT OF FALSE
7.	TRUE	SORT OF TRUE	FALSE	SORT OF FALSE
8.	TRUE	SORT OF TRUE	FALSE	SORT OF FALSE
9.	TRUE	SORT OF TRUE	FALSE	SORT OF FALSE
10.	TRUE	SORT OF TRUE	FALSE	SORT OF FALSE
11.	TRUE	SORT OF TRUE	FALSE	SORT OF FALSE
12.	TRUE	SORT OF TRUE	FALSE	SORT OF FALSE
13.	TRUE	SORT OF TRUE	FALSE	SORT OF FALSE
14.	TRUE	SORT OF TRUE	FALSE	SORT OF FALSE
15.	TRUE	SORT OF TRUE	FALSE	SORT OF FALSE
16.	TRUE	SORT OF TRUE	FALSE	SORT OF FALSE
17.	TRUE	SORT OF TRUE	FALSE	SORT OF FALSE
18.	TRUE	SORT OF TRUE	FALSE	SORT OF FALSE
19.	TRUE	SORT OF TRUE	FALSE	SORT OF FALSE
20.	TRUE	SORT OF TRUE	FALSE	SORT OF FALSE
21.	TRUE	SORT OF TRUE	FALSE	SORT OF FALSE
22.	TRUE	SORT OF TRUE	FALSE	SORT OF FALSE
23.	TRUE	SORT OF TRUE	FALSE	SORT OF FALSE
24.	TRUE	SORT OF TRUE	FALSE	SORT OF FALSE
25.	TRUE	SORT OF TRUE	FALSE	SORT OF FALSE

THE "WORRY LIST"

FOR EACH OF THE FOLLOWING STATEMENTS, CIRCLE ON YOUR ANSWER SHEET WHETHER YOU THINK IT IS TRUE, SORT OF TRUE, FALSE, OR SORT OF FALSE.

1. Right now my main worry is about having been sexually abused and how I can learn to handle my feelings about it.
2. One of my main worries is getting along with my mother (caretaker) and family.
3. I worry that sexual abuse could happen to me again.
4. I feel angry a lot that I have been sexually abused.
5. I feel different from other people because I have been sexually abused.
6. I worry that my boyfriend (girlfriend) or later my husband (wife) will not like me as well because I have been sexually abused.
7. I worry that maybe the abuse was my fault.
8. I feel angry with my mother (caretaker) and family because they did not stop the abuse.
9. I have trouble saying no to people who try to give me bad touches or sexually abuse me.
10. I think things might have been better if I never told about the abuse.
11. I worry that other people will think I am "damaged" because I have been sexually abused.
12. I feel bad that I also have some good feelings toward the person who sexually abused me (as well as angry, bad feelings toward him [her]).
13. I worry that other people, even my family, blame me for the abuse because I did not tell about it sooner.
14. I feel helpless sometimes to keep sexual abuse from happening to me again.

THE "WORRY LIST" ANSWER SHEET

For each statement, circle the answer you think is right. Decide if you think it is TRUE, SORT OF TRUE, FALSE, or SORT OF FALSE. TRUE means you agree with the sentence. SORT OF TRUE means that you think some things about it are true, but you do not agree completely. FALSE means you do not think the sentence is true, and you disagree with it. SORT OF FALSE means you think some things about the sentence are not true, and you do not completely disagree with it. Make sure you are on the right number of the statement before you circle your answer.

1.	TRUE	SORT OF TRUE	FALSE	SORT OF FALSE
2.	TRUE	SORT OF TRUE	FALSE	SORT OF FALSE
3.	TRUE	SORT OF TRUE	FALSE	SORT OF FALSE
4.	TRUE	SORT OF TRUE	FALSE	SORT OF FALSE
5.	TRUE	SORT OF TRUE	FALSE	SORT OF FALSE
6.	TRUE	SORT OF TRUE	FALSE	SORT OF FALSE
7.	TRUE	SORT OF TRUE	FALSE	SORT OF FALSE
8.	TRUE	SORT OF TRUE	FALSE	SORT OF FALSE
9.	TRUE	SORT OF TRUE	FALSE	SORT OF FALSE
10.	TRUE	SORT OF TRUE	FALSE	SORT OF FALSE
11.	TRUE	SORT OF TRUE	FALSE	SORT OF FALSE
12.	TRUE	SORT OF TRUE	FALSE	SORT OF FALSE
13.	TRUE	SORT OF TRUE	FALSE	SORT OF FALSE
14.	TRUE	SORT OF TRUE	FALSE	SORT OF FALSE

CHAPTER 9

References

Anthony, E., & Cohler, B. (1987). *The Invulnerable Child.* New York: Guilford.

Anthony, E., & Koupernick, C. (Eds.). (1974). *The Child in His Family: Children at Psychological Risk.* New York: Wiley & Sons.

Atler, M. V. D. (1991). The darkest secret. *People, 6,* 88-92.

Berkowitz, I., & Sugar, M. (1975). Indications and contraindications for adolescent group psychotherapy. In M. Sugar (Ed.), *The Adolescent in Group and Family Therapy.* New York: Brunner/Mazel.

Berliner, L., & Wheeler, R. (1987). Treating the effects of sexual abuse on children. *Journal of Interpersonal Violence, 2,* 415-434.

Bly, N. (1993). *Oprah: Up Close and Down Home.* New York: Zebra.

Briere, J. (1991). *Treating Victims of Child Sexual Abuse.* San Francisco: Jossey-Bass.

Briere, J., & Runtz, M. (1987). Post-sexual abuse trauma: Data and implications for clinical practice. *Journal of Interpersonal Violence, 2,* 367-379 .

Burgess, A., Groth, A., & Holmstrom, L. (1978). *Sexual Abuse of Children and Adolescents.* Lexington, MA: D. C. Heath.

Cohen, J., & Mannarino, A. (1996). A treatment outcome study for sexually abused preschool children: Initial findings. *Journal of the American Academy of Child and Adolescent Psychiatry, 35,* 42-50.

Connors, C. (1978). *Connors Rating Scale.* Odessa, FL: Psychological Assessment Resources.

Corder, B. F. (1987). Planning and leading adolescent therapy groups. In P. A. Keller & S. R. Heyman (Eds.), *Innovations in Clinical Practice: A Source Book* (Vol. 6, pp. 177-196). Sarasota, FL: Professional Resource Exchange.

Corder, B. F. (l994). *Structured Adolescent Psychotherapy Groups.* Sarasota, FL: Professional Resource Press.

Corder, B. F., & Haizlip, T. (1989). The role of mastery experiences in therapeutic interventions for children dealing with acute trauma: Some implications for treatment of sexual abuse. *Psychiatric Forum, 15,* 57-68.

Corder, B. F., Haizlip, T., & DeBoer, P. (1990). A structured, time limited therapy group for sexually abused pre-adolescent girls. *Child Abuse and Neglect, 36,* 243-252.

Corder, B. F., Whiteside, R., & Cornwall, T. (1984). Techniques for increasing effectiveness of cotherapy functioning in adolescent psychotherapy groups. *International Journal of Group Psychotherapy, 34,* 643-654.

Corder, B. F., Whiteside, R., & Haizlip, T. (1980). A study of curative factors in group psychotherapy with adolescents. *International Journal of Group Psychotherapy, 31,* 341-354.

Corder, B. F., Whiteside, R., & Haizlip, T. (1986). Biofeedback, cognitive training, and relaxation techniques as multimodal adjunctive therapy for hospitalized adolescents. *Adolescence, 21,* 339-346.

Corder, B. F., Whiteside, R., & Vogel, M. (1977). A therapeutic game for structuring and facilitating group psychotherapy with adolescents. *Adolescence, 47,* 261-286.

Finkelhor, D. (1987). The sexual abuse of children: Current research reviewed. *Psychiatric Annals, 17,* 233-241.

Finkelhor, D., & Browne, A. (1986). Initial and long term effects: Conceptual framework. In D. Finkelhor (Ed.), *Sourcebook on Child Sexual Abuse.* Beverly Hills, CA: Sage.

Finkelhor, D., Hotaling, G., & Lewis, I. (1990). Sexual abuse in a national survey of adult men and women: Prevalence, characteristics, and risk factors. *Child Abuse and Neglect, 14,* 28-29.

Friedrich, W., Gambsch, P., & Damon, L. (1992). The Child Sexual Behavior Inventory: Normative and clinical comparisons. *Psychoassessment, 4,* 303-321.

Gillis, R., Reynolds, C., & Richmond, B. (1993). *Revised Children's Manifest Anxiety Scale.* Los Angeles: Western Psychological Services.

James, B. (1989). *Treating Traumatized Children.* Lexington, MA: Lexington Books.

James, B., & Nasjleti, M. (1994). *Treating Sexually Abused Children and Their Families.* Palo Alto, CA: Consulting Psychologists Press.

Kovacks, M. (1992). *Children's Depression Inventory.* San Antonio, TX: Psychological Corporation.

Mayer, A. (1982). *Incest: A Treatment Manual for Therapy With Victims and Offenders.* Holmes Beach, FL: Learning Publications.

Mayer, A. (1984). *Sexual Abuse: Causes, Consequences and Treatment of Incestuous and Pedophilic Acts.* Holmes Beach, FL: Learning Publications.

Naglieri, J., LeBuffe, P., & Pfeiffer, S. (1992). *Devereux Scale of Psychopathology.* San Antonio, TX: Psychological Corporation.

Nasjleti, M. (1980). Suffering in silence: The male incest victim. *Child Abuse, 59,* 269-275.

National Center for Child Abuse and Neglect. (1981). *Study Findings: National Study of Incidence and Severity of Child Abuse and Neglect.* Washington, DC: Author.

Pines, M. (1984). Resilient children: A conversation with Michael Rutter. *Psychology Today, 18,* 57-65.

Porter, R., & Cattell, R. (1984). *Children's Personality Questionnaire.* San Antonio, TX: Psychological Corporation.

Rutter, M. (1978). Early sources of security and competence. In J. Brunner & A. Gaston (Eds.), *Human Growth and Development.* Oxford, England: Clarendon Press.

Scheinberg, M., True, F., & Fraenkel, P. (1994). Treating the sexually abused child: A recursive, multimodal program. *Family Process, 33,* 263-276.

Schetky, P., & Green, A. (1988). *Child Sexual Abuse: A Handbook for Health Care and Legal Professionals.* New York: Brunner/Mazel.

Sgroi, S. (Ed.). (1982). *Handbook of Clinical Intervention in Child Sexual Abuse.* Lexington, MA: Lexington Books.

Strobel, C., & Glueck, B. (1973). Biofeedback treatment in medicine and psychiatry: An ultimate placebo. *Seminars in Psychiatry, 5,* 379-393.

Terr, L. (1991). Childhood traumas: An outline and overview. *American Journal of Psychiatry, 148,* 10-20.

Yates, A. (1991). Child sexual abuse. In J. Wiener (Ed.), *Textbook of Child and Adolescent Psychiatry.* Washington, DC: American Psychiatric Press.

THE SESSIONS

TIME-LIMITED GROUP THERAPY FOR
SEXUALLY ABUSED CHILDREN,
ADOLESCENTS, AND TEENS

The remainder of this book contains instructions, didactic content, and supplemental materials for each of the 15 to 16 sessions for children ages 6 to 9 and 10 to 12 (Chapters 10 and 11), and for each of the 12 sessions for adolescents and teens ages 13 and older (Chapters 12 and 13). There are two chapters devoted to 6- to 12-year-olds, and two devoted to teens. The sessions themselves are laid out in Chapters 10 and 12 and, for ease in photocopying, materials needed for those sessions are included in Part IV. Group leaders should include time for reviewing and photocopying these materials during their group preparation each week. Each session's *Materials* section suggests coloring book or activity book pages needed for that particular group session (see below).

In the case of the coloring/activity "books," we have found that distributing a few pages at a time works best. A pocket folder for each member, with one side for finished work and the other for that not yet completed, is an efficient method of organizing many loose sheets of paper. Children always appreciate receiving a completed folder of their work during the last "graduation" session. Because every group is different, it is impossible to be completely specific about which pages apply to each session. Sometimes discussions or other group activities are more important, and therapists may find that they do not use every page of the coloring book. For this reason we have provided a guide to the coloring book and page contents and homework assignments in Chapter 11 (for younger groups). There is also a guide to the activity book and homework assignments for older groups in Chapter 13.

GROUP FORMAT

Each session, although described in detail, is flexible enough to allow for individual circumstances. The session's purpose and required materials are listed at the beginning of each section. With allowances made for levels of development, maturity, and articulateness, a typical session uses the following format:

1. Name practice (first two to three sessions).
2. Role selection (each member selects a specific role for the session from a "role basket" or envelope).
3. Homework collected and "graded" by group or by therapist.
4. Therapist's introduction and implementation of the session's group task.
5. Group chants and cheers for cognitive reinforcement of session's specific learning task.
6. Summarization by the member who has chosen the *Summarizer* role. The *Summarizer* verbalizes the goals of the group, tasks of the session, what she or he learned, what she or he liked best, and what she or he feels needs to be extended into the next session.
7. Positive feedback or compliments, during which the member with the *Complimenter* role gives each person a compliment about her or his participation in the group during that session.
8. Refreshments and clean-up, which promote social skills, reduce anxiety, and symbolize giving and sharing among group members.
9. Homework described and assigned.
10. Positive feedback good-byes, in which the group member assigned the *Hostess (Host)* role stands with the therapist at the door, shaking each member's hand and relating what the hostess (host) liked best about each member's participation.

PARENTAL INVOLVEMENT

As noted in Chapter 6, parent/caretaker participation usually begins after the initial sessions to allow the members to adjust to the group's format. Each parent/caretaker is instructed to sit close to her or his child, to listen to her or his comments, encourage drawings and tasks, and to help with "chants" and "homework" after the session. In addition to providing encouragement and support, the parent's or caretaker's attendance at these sessions also gives the child "permission" to verbalize her or his feelings. In our younger groups, parents/caretakers usually attend every other session. In older groups, they attend every third session. In the following session descriptions we have indicated where parental/caretaker attendance is particularly helpful; however, therapists will want to use their judgment and adjust each group's schedule according to the specific needs of its members and their parents or caretakers.

GOALS FOR STRUCTURED GROUP THERAPY

Because it is so important to keep treatment goals in mind, we reiterate them here before proceeding with individual session contents. Every activity described in the following chapters has been designed to facilitate achievement of one or more specific goals. Therapists helping clients to work toward these goals are providing valuable tools — not only for trauma recovery and prevention of further abuse, but also for living full and satisfying lives.

The goals are:

- *To improve cognitive and emotional mastery of the trauma* by providing emotional catharsis; intellectual understanding of abuse; relaxation, coping, and communication techniques; and positive alliances with adults who understand and peers who have shared the same experience.
- *To build self-esteem* through cognitive relabeling and a series of positive experiences and activities that teach social skills and encourage self-expression.
- *To improve problem-solving skills* for many kinds of situations, including dealing with potentially abusive situations and finding successful ways to meet one's needs.
- *To promote improved communications* within families, foster-families, and in-group living settings (but especially between parent/caretaker and child), which include negotiation skills, behavioral goals, limit-setting and reward patterns, nonhurtful ways to address problems, and understanding and supporting the developmental tasks of children and adolescents.

It is our belief that children and adults who have been exposed to techniques for achieving these goals — intellectual and emotional mastery, self-esteem, problem-solving, and improved communication with their families — will come to resemble more closely those who are labeled "invulnerable" and "resilient."

CHAPTER 10

Groups for Sexually Abused Children Ages 6 to 9 and 10 to 12

SESSION ONE

Purpose

To familiarize members with group format, alleviate anxiety, build expectations for participation and behavior, and initiate cognitive relabeling and desensitization.

Materials Needed

Pretest (Form GM), if not previously administered, and pretest answer sheets, one per member; The "Worry List" if teen version of pretest is used, one per member (see Chapter 8); pencils or crayons; clipboards; soft foam ball; and refreshments.

Format

1. Therapists' introduction/discussion.
2. Critter "Name Game" to introduce members to one other.
3. Pretesting, if necessary.
4. "Cheers and Chants" for positive self-concept and cognitive behavior modification.
5. Refreshments for social skills and nurturing.
6. Clean-up for closure.
7. Positive reinforcement good-byes by therapists.

Contents of Session One

1. *Therapist Introduction/Discussion.* Defining the group as one for sexually abused children, the therapists introduce themselves as people who work with children who have been sexually abused. Most groups will be composed of children who have been referred following investigation and confirmation of abuse, placement decisions, and initial counseling for trauma; nevertheless, it is still essential to define sexual abuse to the group. For example:

"We are (names), and we work with children of all ages who have been sexually abused. You know that sexual abuse means that another person has used your body or made you use theirs in a sexual way that ended up making you feel confused and bad. And that is not the right way to show any kind of love feelings to someone your age. In this group we are going to talk about your feelings about the abuse, learn how to keep yourself safe, learn all the true facts about abuse, learn all the good and strong things about yourselves, and have a good time learning, getting to know each other, and playing together."

2. *Name Learning Exercise* (develops group cohesion, lowers anxiety). "First thing, let's get to know each other's names by playing a game. We'll go around the room and say our names and pick a "critter" (such as an animal, insect, reptile, or bird) that has a name starting with the same letter as ours. I will be [Dr. Corder Camel]." Children each choose a critter that has a name starting with the same letter as their own first name (Betsy Bat, Helen Horse, etc.). You may want to have some names of animals, insects, birds, and reptiles ready and even some pictures of those with which the group may not be familiar. When we began these groups we were sometimes stuck for a critter name when a child refused to use easy or obvious ones; therefore we include suggestions for letters of the alphabet on page 52.

    After the names have been picked, the foam ball is tossed randomly around the room from child to child. For the first round, the child simply says her (his) name and critter, and throws the ball to any other person in the group, who then jumps up and says her (his) own name and critter (Alice Antelope, etc.).

    For the next rounds, the child says her (his) name and animal and then repeats the name and animal of the person to whom she (he) plans to throw the ball, who repeats the process.

3. *Pretesting.* Following introductions, therapists may wish to introduce the pretest (see Chapter 8) which, along with refreshments and learning a group "cheer," will finish the first session. This task can be included as part of the therapists' description of the group's purposes and described as "going over some of your ideas about some of the things we will be talking about in the group." The drawback of administering the pretest during this first session is that it takes time away from interactions and activities more enjoyable to children. On the other hand, it can also serve to stimulate discussion and focus attention on the issue, and it saves a tremendous amount of time when compared to individual pregroup administrations.

    Introduction of the pretest might sound like this:

    "We are going to read to you some things that people sometimes think about sexual abuse. What we want to know is what YOU think about every one of these sentences. We will read out loud each sentence, and you will draw a circle around the word (on your answer sheet) that tells if you think that the sentence is true, not true, or you're not sure or you don't really know.

    "Let's practice on something really easy. Suppose the first sentence says: 'I came here today with my mother.' You would circle: true, not true, or not sure. What would each of you circle? Now this second one is harder. But you can put down what you really feel. Suppose the second sentence says: 'I wanted to come to this group today.' Circle true, not true, or not sure. Excellent. Now I will read out loud the sentences and you circle your answer, whether you think the sentence is true, not true, or you're not sure or you don't really know."

    Chapter 8 contains copies of the pre- and posttest which can be reproduced. Please note that we have usually used the longer teen (PT) version for children aged 10 and over; however, either version is appropriate.

4. *Cheer* (initiates desensitization and cognitive relabeling). "Now that you're all finished with this worksheet, we're going to do a 'cheer' or 'chant.' That means we say a poem that has something important to remember in it while we clap hands with each other."

For cheers, pair members (using therapist as a partner if numbers are uneven) and repeat the cheer emphasizing the words in rhythm with clapping. Each person (a) claps hands on knees, palms down, (b) then claps own hands together, (c) then claps hands, palms out with their partner, (d) then claps own hands together, (e) then claps own knees, palms down, and begins again.

Even the "rhythmically challenged" can eventually handle this exercise, which is a more complicated version of "patty-cake." However, it is probably a good idea to practice this with your co-therapist or a willing co-worker so it will be easy to demonstrate it for the group.

Cheer #1, Session One (clap in emphasis with capitalized words):

> Lots of PEOPLE have been ABUSED.
> We know THAT 'cause we heard it in the NEWS.
> It's NOT my fault abuse happened to ME.
> I'm a good PERSON everybody will AGREE.

5. *Refreshments.* These should be simple. Their purpose is to lower anxiety, teach social skills, and demonstrate caring and giving, particularly to those children who have not experienced them sufficiently or appropriately. Refreshments are usually a plate of cookies and paper cups of juice or soda. In subsequent sessions refreshments will be served by the child or children who draw the *Hostess (Host)* role at the beginning of the group session. Therapists may invite children to help during this first session. Dietary or religious restrictions for any group member should have already been explored by therapists in initial referral planning.

6. *Clean-Up.* Cleaning up may be shared by the group or defined as part of the role of the person drawing the *Hostess (Host)* card. This activity provides closure and may help to develop a sense of ownership of the group and its process.

7. *Ending the Session: Positive Feedback Good-Byes* (build self-esteem, encourage mastery, enhance group cohesion). The therapist stands at the door (in later sessions with the child or children who have picked the designated role of *Complimenter* or *Hostess [Host]*), shakes each child's hand, and says, "Good-bye Sally Seal, I am looking forward a lot to seeing you next week." The therapist then adds a compliment (positive feedback): a simple positive statement about the child's behavior in the group. In later sessions, these statements will be a repetition of positive feedback statements given by members in the *Complimenter* role.

This form of saying good-bye helps to define some of the "good touches" and appropriate forms of caring that will be discussed in later sessions. It is an opportunity to give "positive strokes" or feedback to members concerning their participation in the group and to set expectations for appropriate group behaviors.

SUGGESTED CRITTERS FOR THE "NAME GAME"

A: armadillo, antelope, anteater, alligator, ant
B: bat, buzzard, bull, bird, butterfly
C: cat, cougar, crocodile, camel
D: dog, deer, duck, dolphin, dinosaur
E: elk, eagle, elephant, ermine
F: frog, fish, falcon, fawn, finch
G: gnat, gazelle, giraffe, gorilla, grasshopper
H: horse, hippo, hedgehog, hornet, hummingbird
I: insect, ibis, iguana
J: jaguar, jackrabbit, jay, jackal
K: kangaroo, kingfisher, kiwi
L: lamb, leopard, lion, llama, lobster
M: moose, mink, marlin, mastodon, mockingbird
N: nightingale, newt, newfoundland (dog)
O: otter, owl, orangutan, oriole, ostrich
P: panda, panther, parrot, penguin, pigeon
Q: quail
R: rabbit, raccoon, ram, raven, reindeer
S: sable, sandpiper, seal, seahorse, sparrow
T: tiger, tern, turtle
U: unicorn
V: vole, vulture, vicuña
W: whale, walrus, wren, weasel, woodchuck
X: xeme (an arctic gull)
Y: yak, yellow jacket
Z: zebra

SESSION TWO

Purpose

To promote group cohesion, alleviate anxiety, set expectations for group behavior, begin self-identification as sexually abused and reduction of feelings of "differentness," and practice mastery, assertiveness, social skills, and problem solving.

Materials Needed

Foam ball, role basket (see description below), easel/markers or chalkboard/chalk, *"Wouldn't It Be Nice"* coloring book: cover page A1 through page A6 (one each per member), clipboards or drawing surfaces, pencils, crayons, Homework Assignment #1 (one per member), and refreshments.

Format

1. "Name Game." Introduction of parents/caretakers if they are attending.
2. Therapists restate group goals and introduce session.
3. Role selection and therapists' description of roles.
4. Setting up group rules.
5. Announcing and beginning a group task (coloring book exercise to illustrate the idea that when bad things happen to good children it is not their fault).
6. Cheer.
7. Summary by member who has drawn *Reminder* role.
8. Compliments by member who has drawn *Complimenter* role.
9. Refreshments.
10. Clean-up.
11. Passing out homework.
12. Positive feedback good-byes.

Contents of Session Two

1. *"Name Game."* Described in Session One, the "Name Game" is played at the beginning of Session Two to promote group cohesion and reduce tension. Members use the same critter names as in Session One. If parents and caretakers are present, each group member should introduce the adult accompanying her (him). At the therapists' discretion, parents may also participate in the "Name Game."
2. *Introduction of Session and Restatement of Goals.* To promote intellectualization and set expectations, therapists use statements from Session One to restate group goals.
3. *Drawing a Role from the "Role Basket."* This activity provides practice in mastery, assertiveness, problem solving, and social skills. After names are learned in the "Name Game," each member selects the role she (he) will take in this session from role cards (see next page) placed face down in a small basket or box. Some therapists like to tape the roles on members' shirts during the first few group sessions, and most like to be sure there are equal numbers of role cards and members. Some suggested roles and their functions are:

Hostess (Host) (there may be two cards with this role):	*Hostesses (Hosts)* give out refreshments and shake each member's hand at departure, saying the member's name and critter name. With the therapists' help, they also repeat one of the "compliments" given to that member in the group, for example, "Good-bye Sally Seal. We liked the way you talked a lot in the group today."
Rules Enforcer:	Reminds people in the group of the group rules and points out when someone is breaking a rule.
Homework Person:	Passes out homework, collects it, and helps with "grading."
Group Helper:	Helps anyone who needs help with drawings or tasks in the group. Therapists call on this person when they see that another member needs assistance.
Group Actor(s):	In future sessions, one or two role-playing cards may be included. These members are to do any initial role-playing exercises that are part of group tasks, although more members may be involved in role-play in the session.
Group Neatness Officer:	This member is responsible for leading the group in clearing the room and returning materials after the session.
Reminder or Summarizer:	At the end of the session, with help from the therapists, the *Reminder* verbalizes "what we did in the group today, and what we learned."
Complimenter:	This task may be combined with that of the *Reminder* in older children's groups, or with that of *Hostess (Host)*. This member's role is to go around the group and tell each member, "What I liked about what you said or did in the group today" (with assistance from therapists if necessary).

4. *Setting Up Group Rules.* This task encourages problem solving, encourages assertiveness, and improves group cohesion. Using easel or chalkboard, the group leader initiates the task. "In this group we will have rules that will help us use our time well, make sure everyone gets to participate, and make sure nobody gets hurt feelings. We already have one rule that the leaders have suggested. Now what are some other rules you would like us to follow to make this a good, fun, but hard-working group?"

The leaders have written out their rule: "Everyone will try all the games and workbooks we use in the group." If there are no suggestions from the group, the leader might say, "What do you think the rules should be about talking to other people, except your mother or caretaker, about what goes on in this group?" "What rules would make it easy for everyone to get a chance to talk?" "Should we make a rule about cleaning up?"

Rules should be few and simple, but should include confidentiality ("No one will talk about what we say here in the group except to your mother or caretaker so that we can feel free to say whatever we want to"). Be sure to add that group leaders might sometimes have to talk to a parent/caretaker or adult if they believe a member is doing something hurtful or is being hurt in some way, so that it can be stopped.

Rules should always include being respectful while others are talking. A rule about cleaning up and using the facility reinforces responsibility. It is helpful with younger children to insist that everyone should go to the bathroom before the session, since children sometimes use trips to the bathroom as tension relievers when group tasks are difficult for them. With many of our youngest groups it has been part of the routine to stand outside the door while all members are ushered to the bathroom before the group. They are told, "Everybody has to try to go to the bathroom, even if they don't think they need to, because we can't leave the group room after we get started."

5. *Session's Group Task: Introducing Coloring Book.* Group leaders may say, "Remember what we said about the reasons we are here: to learn that the abuse was not your fault, to understand all the facts we know about abuse, to remember that many, many people have been abused and you are not alone, and to learn what a good and strong person you are and how you can take care of yourself and get help from others so you won't be sexually abused again. One way we're going to do this is to learn from a special coloring book, like this one, that each one of you will have. You'll get a few pages of it at a time, and get to keep it after the group is over. Let's color the first page and put your name on it." The group will color a few pages of the book at a time during the following sessions. Selected pages will reflect the subjects of the session's specific task.

As noted earlier, each child should have a clipboard or stiff drawing surface slightly larger than the book's page size, and a pencil and package of crayons to use while sitting on the floor in an informal manner. If this is not possible, a large table may be necessary, although tables make the atmosphere more formal and less enjoyable.

The purpose of this activity is to help members begin to identify themselves as sexually abused in ways that promote desensitization, reduce feelings of "differentness," and build group cohesiveness. The therapist states: "While you are coloring the first page, we will go around the group, and each person will say their name and critter and say who abused her (him)." ("I'm Denise Deer, and my daddy abused me.") Using the coloring activity during this disclosure appears to lower anxiety considerably while it helps children to identify themselves and their abusers. Therapists introduce themselves as, "I'm Dr. _____. I have worked with lots and lots of children who have been abused, and I know some things that help them which I am going to teach you." Or, if it is true and therapists wish to share the information with the group, they might say, "I'm Dr. _____, and I was abused when I was a child by my _____. I have learned to handle my feelings about being abused, I feel good about myself, and I know how to take care of myself. I am going to help teach you some of these same things I have learned."

After handing out coloring book pages and initiating the round of abuse disclosure, the leader might say, "Today we are going to talk about how sometimes bad things happen to good people. It isn't their fault; it's just the way things are. There ARE some things we can do to help take care of ourselves and try to help us keep bad things from happening. That's what we are going to learn from these pages. While you color the pages, I'll read what they say." (Therapist reads pages A3 to A6 of the coloring book.) During this activity, therapists compliment and support coloring activities. They may also ask the *Group Helper* to assist in this activity.

"These pages are about getting sick, even though you didn't do anything to deserve it. Sexual abuse is a lot like that. Older people should know better than to abuse children, so it is not your fault that this happened to you. Sexual abuse happens to many people. Some people who study about abuse say that one in every five girls has been sexually abused. This means that probably somebody in your class at school, or in your church, or in your neighborhood has also been abused, even though you might not know about it. Let's go around the group and have everybody tell about something *besides* abuse that happened to her (him) that was not her (his) fault. It could be like when you had an accident and were hurt, or when you got sick, or even when somebody you know got sick and died. After we do that, let's all go around the group and say, 'I have been abused, but it's never the child's fault, it's the older person's fault. It was not my fault.'" This reinforces cognitive relabeling and intellectualization.

6. *Cheer* (desensitization, cognitive relabeling). "Now that you're all finished coloring, we're going to do a Cheer. That means we say a poem that has something important to remember in it while we clap hands with each other. Repeat cheer from Session One:

> Lots of PEOPLE have been ABUSED.
> We know THAT 'cause we heard it in the NEWS.
> It's NOT my fault abuse happened to ME.
> I'm a good PERSON everybody will AGREE.

7. *Summary by the Reminder* (intellectualization, group cohesion, drill in cognitive behavioral modification). The leader assists the member who drew the role of *Summarizer* or *Reminder* by saying, "First tell something we learned in the group today." If she (he) is hesitant, therapists can help by starting: "We learned that abuse is not the child's fault. It is the fault of the _____, because he (she) is older and knows better and knows it is against the law for an adult to abuse a child."

8. *Positive Strokes or Compliments* (building self-esteem, feelings of mastery, reinforcing positive behaviors). The member with the *Complimenter* role, with therapists' help, goes around the group and tells something she (he) liked about what each person did or said.

9. *Refreshments* (group cohesion, nurturance, building social skills). The *Hostess (Host)* takes charge of this activity and models polite eating, "please" and "thank-you."

10. *Clean-Up* (see Session One).

11. *Passing Out Homework* (mastery, intellectualization, drill in cognitive behavioral modification, positive interaction with mother/caretaker). "Here is some homework for you and your parent or the person who takes care of you. It is different from other homework, because your parent or helping person has to read it out loud, and you have to help her or him fill it out if she or he doesn't know the answers. If your parent or helping person doesn't have time to do this with you or you can't get them to finish it, that's okay, too. But we have told your parents and caretakers to help you with the homework, and they probably will do it, especially if you remind them."

    The therapist and group often review homework together, with therapists reminding members of the "right" answers. (Homework Assignment #1 appears on page D3.)

12. *Positive Feedback Good-Byes* (see Session One).

SESSION THREE

Purpose

Mastery practice, learning coping and problem-solving skills, intellectualization, acknowledging and removing feelings of "differentness," behavioral modification drill, self-esteem, social skills, and relabeling.

Materials Needed

Role basket, homework "gradebook," coloring book pages A7 to A10, pencils, crayons, clipboards, refreshments, and Homework Assignment #2.

Format

1. Role selection by each member.
2. *Homework Grader* and therapist go over homework from last session.
3. Announcing and beginning group task (coloring book pages A7-A10: why adults sexually abuse children, abuse is against the law, good and bad secrets, what children can do).
4. Summarization.
5. Positive feedback and compliments.
6. Chant.
7. Refreshments.
8. Clean-up.
9. Passing out homework and review of answers.
10. Positive feedback good-byes.

Contents of Session Three

In the following session descriptions we elaborate only on activities newly introduced for that session. Where activities are not described, please refer to their discussion in previous session content descriptions.

1. *Role Selection.* Therapists greet members and ask them to select a role for the session.
2. *Homework Grader and Therapist Go Over Homework from Last Sessions.* Homework assignments provide two opportunities: practice of didactic material presented in the previous session, and interaction with parents or caretakers concerning the group's work. The "grading" provides drill and reinforcement of concepts, development of intellectualization as a coping mechanism, and positive feedback for members who have attempted the task.

   The grader asks each person if she (he) completed the homework with her (his) parent or helping person and keeps a little "gradebook" with the members' names and grades. The gradebook, which can be a small spiral notebook, is then returned to the therapist for use next session by a different grader. Graders who are slow readers may need help handling this task. The "Grades" are:

S = Satisfactory (child ASKED parent/caretaker to do homework whether she [he] cooperated or not).

NI = Needs Improvement (child forgot to ask parent to do the work).

A = Child asked for homework to be done, parent/caretaker cooperated by at least trying the items.

In other words, members are evaluated not so much for their correct answers but according to their efforts to involve a parent/caretaker. When a member "forgets" to request assistance from her (his) parent or helping person more than once, therapists should explore whether the child is afraid of her (his) parent's/caretaker's reaction, or whether the parent/caretaker has negative feelings about participation.

Leaders may offer to discuss this with parents/caretakers and, if homework is a problem for the parent/caretaker, may excuse the child from homework until the problem can be resolved. Attendance of parents or helping persons at alternate meetings can be a forum for discussion and support of parents'/caretakers' involvement in homework. This third session, the first in which homework is evaluated, can be a good one for parents' or caretakers' first visit to the group.

3. *Therapist Introduces the Session's Task to Group* (intellectualization, dealing with guilt, improving self-esteem, helping to remove feelings of differentness, introduction of coping skills, mastery practice).

"Today we are going to talk about and color pages that deal with a question that many children ask. 'Why does the abuser do it? Why do adults or older youths abuse children?' We don't know all the answers, but we do know that they have a lot of problems and that there is something wrong with *them* — not with *you* — that makes them do this. Some doctors and other people think that abusers never learned the right way to show their love feelings. They did not learn that adults show sexual love feelings only to other adults. Maybe that was because they were sexually abused themselves as children. Some people think that it is because they feel they are not good enough sexually for a grown person, and that a child will not know the difference. Whatever the reason is, all adults know in their heads that it is not right to sexually abuse a child. The ones who did this to you had real problems in their heads. But that does not excuse them. They knew it is against the law to do these things. It is against the law because it is upsetting and confusing to a child to keep secrets about it in the family, and because children are too young to be able to understand and handle the real adult sexual love feelings they will have when they are grown up. Just as you are too young to work 8 hours a day like adults, your body is also too young for adult sexual love feelings. And just as it is against the law to have children work 8 hours a day, it is against the law to make them do adult sexual love behaviors.

"Let's color these pages and talk about them while we do it. You can ask any questions you want to ask while we are coloring. Then we will put your pages in a folder with your name on it, and you will get to keep the whole coloring book when we are finished."

As children color *"Wouldn't It Be Nice"* pages (suggested: A7 and A9) the therapist reads the *"What We Can Do About It"* pages aloud (A8 and A10), transitioning with "When abuse happened to you, you did not know what to do about it. We are going to talk now about some of the things that you can learn now about helping keep yourself safe."

4. *Summarization. Reminder* and therapist go over what was learned today (some reasons why adults abuse children).

5. *Positive Feedback or Compliments* (self-esteem, cohesion).

6. *Chant* (desensitization, cognitive relabeling). Repeat with rhythmic clapping:

That was THEN, but this is NOW.
I WON'T be abused, and I know HOW.

7. *Refreshments* (cohesion, nurturance, social skills).
8. *Clean-Up* (closure, cohesion, responsibility).
9. *Passing Out Homework and Review of Answers* (drill on tasks, intellectualization, improving relationship with mother/caretaker, developing coping skills).
10. *Positive Feedback Good-Byes* (nurturance, self-esteem, social interaction practice for members).

SESSION FOUR

Purpose

Same as Session Three.

Materials Needed

Role basket, homework gradebook, *Feeling Faces* (one set per member; pages B1-B6), *"Draw-A-Picture" Sheets* (one set per member; pages C1-C8), crayons, pencils, clipboards, small clay balls (five per child), masking tape, coloring book pages A11 through page A14, Homework Assignment #3, and refreshments.

Format

1. Role selection.
2. Homework "grading."
3. Introduction of session task.
4. *Feeling Faces* and *"Draw-A-Picture" Sheets.*
5. Coloring book task (A11 through page A14: the difference between good and bad secrets, safe and unsafe people and situations).
6. Cheer.
7. Summarization.
8. Refreshments and passing out homework.
9. Clean-up.
10. Positive feedback good-byes.

Contents of Session Four

1. *Role Selection.*
2. *Homework "Grading."*
3. *Introduction of Session Task.* "We are going to color some pages which try to answer some questions that lots of children ask. Lots of children wonder, 'Why didn't my parent or someone know about the sexual abuse, and why didn't they stop it?' How many of you had that question on your mind? Raise your hands." (Go around the group and have each child say what she [he] wondered about, and whether she [he] wondered why no one knew what was going on.)

   "One reason that people may not have known is that the abuser often tells children to be careful to keep this a secret. Sometimes the abuser offers something special to you if you don't tell — something that you really want, like a wonderful new toy, or a trip to Disney World. And sometimes the abuser might threaten to hurt you or your parent, or other children in the family if you tell. Or the abuser might say that the family would be really mad at both of you and might make you both leave, or that your parent would be mad at him (her) and might make him (her) leave, and then the family would have no money for food and things. Sometimes abusers even say that it is all your fault and that if you tell, everyone will make you leave the family. Sometimes the abuser doesn't really say anything out loud to you about not telling, but you feel like everyone would blame you for letting it ever happen at all, and you're afraid to tell."

   (Go around the room and have each child give some reasons why she [he] didn't tell anyone at first about the abuse.)

4. *Feeling Faces* (catharsis, verbalization of feelings, losing feelings of differentness, group cohesion). Therapist: "Here are some drawings of people's faces showing some of the feelings that children have when they have been abused. Look through your set of *Feeling Faces*, and let's go over each one of them and the feelings they show. Now think about how you felt when nobody seemed to know about the abuse and didn't stop it. You might have had several of the feelings." (Go around the group, normalizing their feelings by saying to each child, "Alice felt scared and mad, right?" And "Mary, you're holding up cards that say you felt guilty and sad and mad.")

"It looks as if all of you held up cards that showed you had some of the same feelings that other children who have been sexually abused have had. It is normal for you to have had all those feelings, and maybe you still have some of them.

"Now hold up the faces that show how you felt when the person who sexually abused you told you to keep it a secret." (Repeat process of labeling each child's feelings and having her [him] verbalize her [his] agreement, thus normalizing her [his] feelings by labeling them as typical and shared by many other children.)

"Now let's talk about some of the things you can do about these feelings, particularly if you still have a lot of them. First, you could talk to people you trust about the feelings. You could talk with your parent or people in your family, or with the people here in this group. It is important to talk with people you trust, and who will understand about these feelings. Sometimes other children who don't know you very well, don't understand. Who would you tell about these feelings about being abused, and who wouldn't you tell?" (Go around the room and encourage children to keep their discussions about being abused limited to their family, helping adults, and perhaps one best friend whom they feel would understand and not involve a lot of other children who might not understand the feelings or experience.)

"Draw-A-Picture" Sheets — "Another way to get rid of feelings that bother you is to draw pictures about them. Everybody take your pieces of paper with names of some feelings on them, and draw a feeling you'd like to be rid of. It can be an angry feeling, sad feeling, guilty feeling — just choose the colors that remind you of the feeling and make marks or drawings that remind you of it. Make any drawing that reminds you of that feeling. Here is what an angry feeling looks like and feels like to me (demonstrates dark red and black slash marks on page with stars, lightening bolts, etc.). Now everybody make one for the feelings they picked."

After finishing the drawings, give each child five balls of clay and tape the pictures on the wall. "Now everybody throw the clay at the feeling picture, and say something like, "Take that! Get gone you old (sad, angry, guilty) feeling! Take that, you mean thing! I don't have to feel bad about you anymore."

5. *Coloring Book Task* (catharsis, intellectualization, mastery). "Now we're going to color some pages. The first one (page A11) tells about good secrets and bad secrets and how not to keep the bad secrets. Then we will look at some lists of reasons why children don't tell about the abuse right away. The second page (page A13) tells about why parents and other people in the family don't know about the abuse, and don't let themselves believe that it is happening. The main thing we are learning is why children keep abuse a secret, why other people don't know about it or stop it right away, and what a child can do about it. The main thing is you have to keep telling your family, your teacher, your Sunday School teacher, your principal, or even the police, until somebody stops the abuse." (Therapist may read pages A12 and A14 aloud.)

6. *Cheer* (drill, cognitive relabeling):

I didn't KNOW what I should DO.
My PARENT didn't KNOW what I was going THROUGH.
I FELT so BAD, I wanted to SHOUT.
But NOW I understand, and we can WORK it OUT.

7. *Summarization* (drill, intellectualization as a defense, normalization of feelings and reactions, rehearsal of coping and mastery skills).
8. *Refreshments and Passing Out Homework.* This can be a time for reviewing homework, reading it together, and giving answers to new homework questions.
9. *Clean-Up.*
10. *Positive Feedback Good-Byes.*

SESSION FIVE

Purpose

Same as Sessions Three and Four, special emphasis on coping and developing mastery techniques.

Materials Needed

Role basket and cards, homework gradebook, coloring book pages A15 through A18, Homework Assignment #4, and refreshments.

Format

1. Role selection.
2. Homework "grading."
3. Session task — Role-playing: If you had already known what we are learning now in this group.
4. Coloring book (pages A15-A18: Taking care of yourself; telling, even if the abuser threatens you).
5. Cheer.
6. Summarization.
7. Refreshments and passing out homework.
8. Clean-up.
9. Positive feedback good-byes.

Contents of Session Five

1. *Role Selection.*
2. *Homework "Grading."*
3. *Session Task.* "This time we are going to talk about what you could have done differently when the abuse started, IF YOU HAD ALREADY KNOWN WHAT WE ARE LEARNING NOW IN THIS GROUP. When the abuse happened to you, you had little or no help in knowing what to do. While we color and read, let's go over some of the things you could do now or might have done then if you had already been in this group.

   "First, you can learn to know when somebody is acting oddly toward you — no matter who the person is. If someone tries to give you bad touches, or you feel funny or odd about anything that person is asking you to do, there are some things you can do. Let's talk about some of the things someone could do that would make you feel scared or funny. Someone might keep asking you to sit on their lap and hold you real close, patting on your body in a way that made you uncomfortable. Or that person could keep talking about grown-up sex in a lot of detail when you are alone with him (her). What are some of the things the person who abused you did that worried you when he (she) first started the abuse?" (Encourage children to go around the group and answer while they are coloring. This sometimes lowers the anxiety level in the group and allows members to speak with less discomfort. They may give answers such as having been asked to lie down with the person, touching the abuser, or being given baths and touched in their private parts.)

"Now let's talk about some of the things you can do when this happens to you. First you could say, 'No, I'm going to tell my (parent/caretaker, teacher, etc.).' Then you should try to leave and stop being alone with him (her). You should tell another adult about your worry about the abuser. If that person does not get the abuse stopped, keep telling other older people, until finally someone will stop it. If you are really frightened and nobody will stop the abuse, you can dial 911 on the telephone, and the police will stop it."

Role-Play. "Who got the role-play cards from the basket today? Okay. I will help you act out what you can do if you think somebody might be trying to abuse you. One of you will be someone trying to abuse a child, and one will be a child who knows ways to try and stop it. I will whisper in your ear what to say and do. We'll call the little girl Alice, and the abuser will be her Uncle Jim."

Uncle Jim:	You are so cute and pretty, nobody is around and I want to show you how cute you are. Come and sit on my lap and let me give you a big hug, and pats on your little bottom.
Alice:	(LOUD) NO! I don't want to do that!
Uncle Jim:	Well, why not? I'm just trying to be nice and show you how cute you are.
Alice:	No! It makes me feel funny and scared.
Uncle Jim:	Okay. You're just being a silly girl. Come here.
Alice:	No! I'm leaving. And I'm going to tell my mother when she gets back.
Therapist:	Very good. Now suppose Alice's mother doesn't think there's anything wrong with her uncle's behavior, and Uncle Jim keeps trying to do things to her, like touching her and her private parts. She should tell her mother again, and ask her not to ever leave her alone with her Uncle Jim, and then she could tell other people in the family if nothing changes and the abuse keeps on. Name some people she could tell (grandmother, aunt, other adults in her family, teacher, minister, principal, counselor at school).
	Suppose no one did anything for a long time, and Uncle Jim tried to make Alice do something very scary, like touching his private parts or putting his private parts on or in her. She should yell out real loud "NO! I DON'T WANT TO DO THAT. I'M GOING TO TELL ON YOU," and try to run away from him. She might run next door, or to someone in her family if they live close by. If she can't get anyone to help her, she should go to a phone and dial 911. The police will always answer and will get her some help. Let's practice that. One of you will be scared, and I will be the operator at 911.
911 Operator:	Hello 911 police emergency.
Child:	Hello, I'm scared, and somebody is trying to sexually abuse me.
911 Operator:	What is your name and where are you?
Child:	My name is _____ and I am at my house at _____.
911 Operator:	Who is this person, and what are they trying to do to you?
Child:	It is my uncle, and he tried to put his private part in my bottom.
911 Operator:	Are you alone, or is the person who is trying to abuse you there?
Child:	He's upstairs.
911 Operator:	Well, go out on your porch or stand by your front door, and the police will be right there and help you. If your uncle comes out, tell him the police are on their way, and he better get out of there and leave you alone.

"This acting shows us what you can do if somebody . . . anybody . . . tries to abuse you and won't stop. First you tell them 'NO! I DON'T WANT TO,' real loud. Then you say, 'STOP! I'M GOING TO TELL (my mother, the police).' Then you try to leave and get away from them. Go out of the house or next door, or someplace close and have them call your mother and the police. Remember if you use a public phone, you don't have to have money to dial 911. You just dial 911, and the police will answer any time of the day or night and will send help for you."

4. *Coloring Book.* (pages A15-A18: taking care of yourself; telling, even if the abuser threatens you).

5. *Cheer.* "This cheer reminds us of what you should do if somebody tries to give you bad touches and won't stop." Clap your hands and let's practice what you should do:

> First say NO! Then you GO.
> RUN and tell SOMEONE.
> Or call 911.

Steps 6 through 9. See previous sessions.

SESSION SIX

Purpose

Same as previous sessions, with emphasis on catharsis, coping, and building self-esteem.

Materials Needed

Role basket, homework gradebook, *Wanda's Story* (pages D13-D16), *Feeling Faces* (pages B1-B6), pencils, crayons, clipboards, Homework Assignment #5, and refreshments.

Format

1. Role selection.
2. Homework "grading."
3. Session task: *Wanda's Story*.
4. Cheer.
5. Summarization.
6. Refreshments and passing out homework.
7. Clean-up.
8. Positive feedback good-byes.

Contents of Session Six

1. *Role Selection.*
2. *Homework "Grading."*
3. *Session Task: Wanda's Story.* Each member is given a set of the *Feeling Faces*. Therapist reads *Wanda's Story* aloud. Therapist instructs: "While I read the story, you are all going to fill in the blanks and say the feeling she is feeling in the story. And you should each hold up the card that shows how she is feeling. Let's look through the cards and remember what all the feelings are. Remember that sometimes she will be feeling more than one feeling, and you can hold up more than one card. Ready? Here is *Wanda's Story*.
4. *Chant and Cheer* (with clapping):

That was THEN, but this is NOW.
I WON'T be abused, and I know HOW.

Steps 5 through 8. Same as previous sessions.

SESSION SEVEN

Purpose

To provide opportunities for catharsis and identification with others, to alleviate isolation and feelings of differentness, and to build coping mechanisms.

Materials Needed

Role basket, homework gradebook, *My Own Story* (pages D17-D18), *Feeling Faces*, Homework Assignment #6, and refreshments.

Format

1. Role selection.
2. Homework "grading."
3. Session task: *My Own Story.*
4. Cheer.
5. Summarization.
6. Refreshments and passing out homework.
7. Clean-up.
8. Positive feedback good-byes.

Contents of Session Seven

1. *Role Selection.*
2. *Homework "Grading."*
3. *Task for Session: My Own Story.* In this session the therapist goes around the group, reading the story aloud for each member and instructing her/him to fill in the blanks and hold up *Feeling Faces* for her/his own story.
4. *Cheer and Chant:*

> That was THEN, but this is NOW.
> I WON'T be abused, and I know HOW.

Steps 5 through 8. Same as previous sessions.

SESSION EIGHT

Purpose

To provide catharsis and intellectualization.

Materials Needed

Blank sheets of paper, foam balls, coloring book pages A3 through page A20, pencils, crayons, clipboards, tape recorder, easel and markers, Homework Assignment #7, and refreshments.

Format

1. Role selection.
2. Homework "grading."
3. Session tasks: coloring book pages (A3 through page A20: confused feelings about abusers); drawing the abusers.
4. Session tasks: using tape recorder; writing a group letter.
5. Cheer.
6. Summarization.
7. Refreshments and passing out homework.
8. Clean-up.
9. Positive feedback good-byes.

Contents of Session Eight

1. *Role Selection.*
2. *Homework "Grading."*
3. *Session Tasks: Coloring Book Pages.* "Today we are going to talk about feelings about abusers, and what happens to them, and what we would like to see happen to them. First we are going to color pages from the coloring book that tell about sexual abusers and what usually happens to them. Each case is different, and sometimes the court and judges do not handle things the same for every abuser and their families.

   (After coloring): "Sometimes children are left with very angry feelings that they never get to let out. Today let's let some of them out. First draw a picture of the person who abused you on the blank paper. It can be just his (her) face. Now each of you will get some little foam balls that we're going to pretend are rocks. Then we'll take the pictures you draw of your abuser, put them on the wall, and throw "rocks" at them, while we say things like, 'You're a bad person, you deserve to be put in jail!' or 'I'd really like to punish you. Take that, you mean thing!'

   "Even though we might like to, there are laws about hitting people and making them pay by hitting and hurting them for what they did. The courts have to do the punishment. But we can pretend like we did now, and we can say what we think about them in this group, even though we may not get to say it for real, in person."

4. *Session Task: Using Tape Recorder, Writing a Group Letter.* "Today we also have a little tape recorder, and even though this will not be played for real to the abuser, I'd like each of you to think about what you would really like to say to your abuser. We're going to record a message

from each one of you. We'll all hold hands while you're talking, to remind you that nothing is going to happen to you, that we care about you, and that you can say whatever you feel.

"Now we are going to work as a group to write a group letter and pretend that we will send it to each one of your abusers. We won't send the letter unless you *really* want to, and only after we talk it over here and with your parent(s)/caretaker(s). But let's work on a letter together that says what we would all like to say. It would start something like this:

Dear Sexual Abuser:

I have been in a group with other children who have been sexually abused, and we have been learning about why this happens and talking about our feelings. This is what the whole group would like you to know, and what we would like to say to you:

"Let the group compose the rest of the letter. You may make suggestions, such as: 'Now I know it was never my fault, always the adult's fault, no matter how you lied or what you thought.' or 'You don't have control over me now, and I have learned that I can tell people like the police what you are doing, and they will make you stop.'"

5. *Cheer* (with clapping):

I'm a good PERSON,
I'm proud of ME.
I've BEEN through a LOT,
But look how STRONG I have GOT.

Steps 6 though 9. Same as previous sessions.

Purpose

To teach coping, relaxation techniques, and cognitive relabeling techniques.

Materials Needed

Role basket, homework gradebook, biofeedback machines (optional), coloring book pages A21-A22 and A27-A29 (optional), pencils and crayons, clipboards, refreshments.

Format

1. Role selection.
2. Homework "grading."
3. Session task: learning relaxation techniques.
4. Session task: learning cognitive relabeling skills, coloring book (pages A21-A22, A27-A29 what to do about feelings left over even after you tell).
5. Cheer.
6. Summarization.
7. Refreshments.
8. Clean-up.
9. Positive feedback good-byes.

Contents of Sessions Nine and Ten

1. *Role Selection.*
2. *Homework "Grading."*

NOTE: Therapists should review member's charts and medical information to assure that all members are able to perform these simple relaxation exercises safely. Although unlikely, it is possible that some children with unusual medical problems might have difficulty with the tasks. These sessions are also helpful for parents and caretakers.

---

3. *Session Task: Learning Relaxation Techniques.* "Today we are going to learn some ways to handle feelings when they make us unhappy, worried, or sad. Let's go around the group and talk about some of the ways that each of you have tried to let your feelings out so that you can get rid of them." Members may describe talking to others, throwing pillows, crying in their bedrooms, and so forth. Therapists acknowledge and validate each member's contribution.

    "Besides sad and mad feelings, most people also have sort of scared, nervous feelings that make them feel bad, and are hard to talk about in words. Some of the ways we talked about in this group may be good ways for you to handle all of your uncomfortable feelings. But today we are going to learn another special way to handle uncomfortable feelings, called 'Special Relaxation.'

- "First, let's help your body get relaxed. Start with your toes and then your knees, then thighs, stomach, arms, hands, neck, and face. Let's scrunch them up as tightly as possible, keeping each one tight till you count to 10. Now start to let them go limp and relaxed, even letting your mouth hang open and your shoulders slump and fall down. Let's do that three times.
- "Now you are all going to learn to think of a special, quiet, safe, nice place that you can picture in your mind. Let's go around the group and get a special place for each one to picture in their mind. It could be your own bed, or sitting on the beach alone, or sitting in a swing in your yard. Just so it is a nice, quiet, calm, safe place that you enjoy.
- "Now everybody close your eyes and try to 'see' your safe place. Try to feel like you are really there. Don't try to think of anything else or do anything else. Just be there in your quiet, safe place.
- "Now we are going to practice breathing and relaxing. First take three long breaths, and let them out really slowly. Take a deep breath through your nose. Hold it till you count to five, and then let it out really slowly through your nose. Now do this with your eyes closed one time, and at the end, when you let out the air very slowly through your mouth, let your body slump and breathe like you do when you're about to go to sleep.
- "Very good. Now let's try to put it all together. First let's do the body-scrunching and relaxing three times. Then let's do the three deep breaths, holding till you count to five, then letting it out *very* slowly with your eyes closed. At the end of the third breath, sit all slumped over like a rag doll, breathe like you're going to sleep, and think of your special, safe place in your mind. See if you can imagine yourself there, all safe and relaxed.

    "Let's practice a few times, and then go around the room and think of when and where you might want to do this kind of relaxing (for instance, when you are feeling very nervous or upset, you might go to your room and do the relaxing).

    "This type of relaxing usually requires that you be alone, and is hard to do when other people are around. Now we're going to talk about some things that you can do to relax and make yourself feel better, even if you are not alone."

4. *Session Task: Cognitive Relabeling.* "Sometimes you might be in school, or someplace you could not do all the exercises we have practiced here. But you could still help yourself get calm and feel better. Here is what you could do:

- "You might be able to do your deep breathing, if nobody else is close by.
- "In your mind you could picture yourself in your safe place, and sometimes you might be able to close your eyes while you picture yourself there, all safe and calm.
- "You can talk to yourself (not out loud), and say nice things to yourself over and over. Try saying one of our chants like: 'I'm a good person, I'm proud of me. I've been through a lot, but look how strong I have got.' This is really true about everyone here. You are good people, and you should be proud of yourselves. You have been through a lot, but you have gotten stronger, and you know ways to get help for yourself, and things to do to keep yourself safe. Let's practice doing these things without making noise, so that nobody but you would know that you are making yourself feel better." (If deemed necessary and if time allows, use the coloring tasks in the coloring book that discuss confusion, anxiety, and talking to oneself.)

When available, the use of small hand-held biofeedback devices is helpful in teaching these techniques, even to young children, because these devices provide concrete evidence that their relaxation efforts are working. Most biofeedback, galvanic skin response (GSR) measurement, and temperature devices come with relaxation tapes giving directions for exercises similar to those described previously.

5. *Cheer:*

> I MAY have some scared feelings come to ME some DAY,
> But I've LEARNED some ways to make them ALL go AWAY.

Steps 6 through 9. Same as previous sessions.

SESSION ELEVEN

Purpose

To build self-esteem and enhance intellectualization and mastery.

Materials Needed

Role basket, a mirror (hand mirror or larger), coloring book pages A23-A29 (optional), crayons and pencils, clipboards, and refreshments.

Format

1. Role selection.
2. Session task: Mirror, Mirror on the Wall.
3. Relaxation practice.
4. Coloring task (optional, pages A23-A29: more facts about abusers, how children who have been abused can grow up to be happy adults).
5. Cheer.
6. Summarization.
7. Refreshments.
8. Clean-up.
9. Positive feedback good-byes.

Contents of Session Eleven

1. *Role Selection.*
2. *Session Task.* "Do you remember the Queen in the movie *Snow White and the Seven Dwarfs*, who would ask questions to her magic mirror? She would say, 'Mirror, Mirror on the wall, who's the fairest one of all?' The mirror was very honest and would always tell the truth and answer, 'Snow White,' and the Queen would be furious. Today we are going to pretend that there is a Magic Mirror. The mirror always tells the truth. It answers any questions you might have been afraid to ask or that you thought nobody knew the right answer to. Most children have lots of questions about sexual abuse. I will pretend to be the Magic Mirror and answer your questions. Although this is pretend, I will be very honest, like the Magic Mirror. I know lots of things about sexual abuse, because I have talked to many, many children and their families, and I have read lots of studies about abuse that other people have written. If you can't think of a question, I'll whisper one in your ear that other children have asked in the past. After each question, we'll ask the group if they agree with the answer, and whether or not they have thought of that same question." After each question, the therapist will go around the group, asking each member if the answer seemed right to them and whether she (he) had wondered about the same question. Members should be encouraged to discuss any other explanation they have to answer each question, as this may reveal some of the "myths" they have learned about sexual abuse.

   The purpose of this exercise is not to go through each question quickly for each group member, but to provide a structured therapeutic play situation within which the group can discuss anxiety-provoking topics and issues.

The therapist continues: "You have all worked very hard to understand about sexual abuse, and you have gotten stronger and know the abuse was not your fault. So the very first question I want each of you to ask the mirror is (each child take turns holding a hand-held mirror up, or standing in front of a larger mirror, while the therapist stands behind her [him] and answers for the Magic Mirror)":

> "Mirror, Mirror on the wall,
> Who is one of the nicest, strongest girls (boys) of all?"

The therapist then answers: "You are, Mary (Jim). You are one of the nicest, strongest girls (boys) of all. Now what is your next question for me?"

Suggested Questions and Answers for the Child Who Has Difficulty Responding:

> *Note to Therapist:* Remember to change gender as appropriate when working with abused boys or a mixed group.

Question: Will I ever stop feeling so bad about the sexual abuse?
Answer: Your sad and mad feelings will get less and less strong as time passes as you learn lots of ways of dealing with your feelings, and as you understand why this happened, like we are learning in this group.

Question: Why did the abuser pick me instead of somebody else to abuse?
Answer: The abuse is never the child's fault. It is the adult's fault, because adults know a child is not ready to understand this kind of sexual behavior. Nothing you did or said made them abuse you. Sometimes you get picked simply because you are the person easiest for them to abuse, because you live in the same house, or because you are alone with them sometimes. Or maybe they thought they could convince you easily that the abuse was all right, because you are a sweet, trusting person who believed most things that adults told them. Some abusers think that they can do anything they want to their own children. That is not true, because you have the right to keep your body private from anyone, no matter who they are. And it is against the law for *anyone* to sexually abuse you.

Question: Why didn't my mother know I was being abused and stop it?
Answer: Sometimes it is so scary to a mother, that she can't let herself believe that this is really happening in her family. And she may be afraid that if she believes in the abuse, the abuser will leave the family and the family will be without money and help. And the mother may like some things about the abuser, and because she likes him, she cannot believe this could be true. Mothers hate to think that they could pick a husband or boyfriend who would do such a thing to their children, so it is very hard for them to accept the idea that abuse is going on.

Question: Why do some mothers get mad at the children when they tell about the abuse after it has been going on for a while?

Answer: They don't understand how frightened and confused the child is in telling about the abuse, and they may think that you should have told them right away, and that you hid the abuse on purpose. Sometimes they are acting mad because they are just as upset about the whole situation as you are. Every mother wants her child to be safe and does not want her child to be abused. But it is upsetting and scary and confusing for them too, even if they are grown-ups, and sometimes it is hard for them to understand everything about abuse too. It is up to the mother to learn to understand that sexual abuse is never the child's fault. It is the fault of the adult.

Question: When I get older and get married, will my husband be mad at me or like me less because I was sexually abused?

Answer: Not if he is the right kind of husband who really loves you and understands about the difference between sexual love between two adults and sexual abuse between an adult and a child. Most husbands who know this are able to love you even more, because they feel sorry for what you have had to go through. Most husbands either understand, or can learn that it was never your fault, but the adult's fault. And they can learn that many, many children have been sexually abused, not just you. You may have to get some help for him to understand all this, maybe go to a counselor together, but a good husband who loves you will learn to understand all these things.

Question: Should I tell other people, like friends, about the sexual abuse after it has stopped and I feel safe?

Answer: Everything about your body is private. Just like you wouldn't tell everybody about some problem with your body, like being constipated, or if you threw up last night, you wouldn't want to discuss something as personal as sexual abuse with anyone other than your closest friend, your family, or your counselor. Also, many people do not understand about sexual abuse the way that we do. A few people do not understand that it is always the adult's fault, and there might even be some who think that it was partially your fault, because they don't know all the true facts. This will change as more and more people learn about sexual abuse. But you should not be hurt by other people's ignorance. Share this with your very closest friend, who will not discuss private things about you with other people, or with your family or helping adults, like teachers and therapists.

Question: Do you think it is bad that sometimes some parts of the sexual abuse were sort of nice (like hugging and kissing before the real bad touches started), and that I sort of liked those parts before the real abuse started?

Answer: No. Everybody likes to be petted and hugged. It is when this kind of love becomes like adult sexual love (touching your private parts, having you touch theirs, talking about details of sex, and having sex) that you feel uncomfortable. Most healthy normal adults know how to show two kinds of love: grown-up sexual love with their wives or husbands, and a different kind of love with children which is not sexual. They hug and kiss children, and want to take care of them, but don't give bad touches or want to have sex with children. Sexual abusers are not normal people, even though they may look normal on the outside and are nice to you and your family in many other ways.

Question: Is it ever better to keep the abuse secret than to upset the whole family?

Answer: No. It is not good for you to keep the abuse secret, and the family has a responsibility to you to help stop this abuse. Some people think it may be easier to keep quiet, but their feelings and worries are still there bothering them unless they get them out and get the abuse stopped. All mothers say that even though it was hard to hear about the abuse, and that the family had lots of hard things to go through, they did not want their children to continue to be sexually abused.

Question: Am I supposed to forgive the abuser?

Answer: You don't have to forgive abusers. You just don't want to spend a lot of your life and time on hating anybody, because it takes away time from being happy and calm. After you have let all your angry and sad feelings out, you might just not want to think about [the abuser] a lot. Or you don't have to forgive the abuser, but just think of him as a person who was not normal, and who did mean things to you, and who is in many ways a mean, cruel person. The main thing you should remember in thinking about the abuser is that the abuse was never your fault, it was his fault. Sometimes you can understand why people do something, but that does not mean you have to forgive them. But we all have to move on to other parts of our lives, and spending too much time hating somebody keeps us from the fun things about life. That's not the same thing as saying that it was okay for the abuser to abuse you, and that you forgive him for it. You might want to think about it this way: "What the abuser did was wrong, and it was not my fault. I have let out a lot of my angry and sad feelings against him. But I still have some of these feelings, and he deserves them, because he did a wrong thing. I understand now some of the reasons he did what he did, but that doesn't mean I have to forgive him. I have my own life to live and things to look forward to and I'm not going to spend too much time on hating the abuser."

Question: When I get to be a teenager and an adult, and get engaged and get married and am ready to have adult sexual feelings, will I have worries and be scared because I was sexually abused when I was young?

Answer: Sometimes people have some worries, but they can usually be taken care of by talking with their spouse, fiancé, or counselor. These worries can almost always be worked out, especially if you have been in a group like this when you were young and already understand a lot about sexual abuse. Some grown-ups have groups like these, particularly if they were not in one when they were young; they talk together about their feelings about being abused when they were children.

Question: How can I keep my own children from being sexually abused?

Answer: You can talk to them and tell them that they can tell you anything they want, and that you want to talk about anything that happens to them, no matter what it is. You can make them feel like you would try to understand anything they tell you, and that you would not get mad at them about it. And you can teach them the things we learned here about their right to keep their body private, how to learn about bad touches, and what to do if this happens to them.

3. *Relaxation Practice.*

4. *Coloring Book Task.* Various pages can be used to reinforce some of the questions group members have asked the Magic Mirror.
5. *Cheer.*

I'm a good PERSON , I'm proud of ME.
I've BEEN through a LOT, but look how STRONG I've GOT.

Steps 6 though 9. Same as previous sessions.

SESSION TWELVE

Purpose

To provide mastery practice, promote intellectualization, and promote group cohesion.

Materials Needed

Role basket, *Moving On and Getting Stronger Game* (pp. E1-E5) and all materials, and refreshments.

Format

1. Role selection.
2. Session task: *Moving On and Getting Stronger Game* (pp. E1-E5).
3. Relaxation practice.
4. Cheer.
5. Summarization.
6. Refreshments.
7. Clean-up.
8. Positive feedback good-byes.

Contents of Session Twelve

1. *Role Selection.*
2. *Session Task: Moving On and Getting Stronger Game.* Today we are going to play a game, the *Moving On and Getting Stronger Game.* Here is the board and each of you will have a game piece with your name on it to move around the board. You'll throw the die to see how many squares you move, and when you land on one, you will pick a question to answer from the pile of Learning Cards. We're playing this game to make sure we remember lots of things we have learned in this group.

   The object of the game (see materials in Part IV) is not to move as quickly as possible from one question to another, but to promote group discussion. Each question should be answered by the player, who then asks the person on his or her left and right the same question, until the question has been answered by everybody, or until the suggested activity has been completed by each group member.

   Depending on the ages and developmental levels of members, a variation of this game may be constructed by including Knowing Yourself, Understanding Each Other, and Problem- Solving cards from the game for older group members, *The Life Game* (see pp. J3-J28).
3. *Practice Relaxation* (see Sessions Nine and Ten).
4. *Cheer:*

   That was THEN, but this is NOW.
   I WON'T be abused, and I know HOW.

*Steps 5 through 8. S*ame as previous sessions.

SESSION THIRTEEN

Purpose

To enhance cognitive reorganization, mastery practice, and intellectualization.

Materials Needed

Role basket and refreshments.

Format

1. Role selection.
2. Session task: 21-year-old role-play.
3. Relaxation practice.
4. Cheer.
5. Summarization.
6. Refreshments.
7. Clean-up.
8. Positive feedback good-byes.

Contents of Session Thirteen

1. *Role Selection.*
2. *Session Task.* Members are asked to describe themselves as they will be and look when they are 21 years old (e.g., what car they want to drive, where they want to work, what college they went to, what is important to them). Therapists instruct each member to imagine that she (he) is making an important visit to someone and that she (he) will be showing off how well she (he) is doing in her (his) life. Members can imagine themselves all dressed up and what they will be wearing: each child should describe her (his) outfit and the car she (he) drives. To make the fantasy more authentic, try to keep members' visual pictures within realistic bounds (a red Firebird convertible instead of a Rolls Royce, for example, or a job as bank vice-president instead of president of Microsoft, etc.).

   The therapist continues: "Now you are all doing very well for yourselves, doing well in your jobs, and looking very good and successful. This trip we are going to take is to see your abuser for 10 minutes. Think about what you would like to say to that person, now that you have so many nice things going on in your life. What do you think the abuser's life will be like then, and what do you want the abuser to know about your feelings and what has happened? Remember that you are grown, the abuser can't hurt you, and you have even more legal rights than you had as a child."

   Each child should have an opportunity to role-play her (his) visit to the abuser at the abuser's home or office. Members who drew the *Actor* cards from the role basket go first.
3. *Practice Relaxation.*
4. *Cheer:*

I'm a good PERSON, I'm proud of ME.
I've BEEN through a LOT, but look how STRONG I've GOT.

Steps 5 through 8. Same as previous sessions.

SESSION FOURTEEN

Purpose

To practice mastery, intellectualization, and coping; to lose the sense of differentness.

Materials Needed

Role basket, previously unused cards from *Moving On and Getting Stronger Game*, a big cut-out box to serve as TV screen (optional), toy microphone (optional), game show prizes (such as Tootsie Roll pops), and refreshments.

Format

1. Role selection.
2. Session task: *TV Quiz Show Game*.
3. Relaxation practice.
4. Cheer.
5. Summarization.
6. Refreshments.
7. Clean-up.
8. Positive feedback good-byes.

Contents of Session Fourteen

1. *Role Selection.*
2. *Session Task: TV Quiz Show Game*. If not using a toy microphone, provide an object that resembles a microphone. Divide the group into two teams, using your city and county as their names (i.e., The Chapel Hill Team, The Wake County Team). A big box cut out like a TV screen is helpful with the fantasy, but is not critical.

Therapist (in Role of TV Emcee): Today we have our two teams, _____ and _____, who will be competing on our show, *Keeping Yourself Safe and Strong*. We will see how much each team has learned about sexual abuse, how to keep themselves safe, how abuse is not their fault, and how they can handle their feelings about abuse. I'll bet our TV audience and even you two teams did not know that sexual abuse has happened to many famous people who have told magazines and TV shows how they were abused, and how they learned to have a good life and be strong (Atler, 1991; Bly, 1993; see References on pages 43-44). This is a visiting TV star, who has told in interviews about how she was sexually abused as a child. Ms. TV star, do you have a few things to say first?

Second therapist, or therapist taking both roles as emcee and Ms. TV star

Therapist as *TV Star:*	Just a few things. I was sexually abused as a child by relatives, and I had a hard time getting over it. But with some help, I have become a famous person who has been able to make lots of money and have lots of the things that everybody wants to have when they are grown. And I told about the abuse because I didn't want people to think that they were the only ones who had been abused, and to remind them that you can move forward from this, get help (like being in this group), and have a good life.

Using cards not used by the group in the *Moving On and Getting Stronger Game*, each person on the two teams takes turns being asked the questions. The famous guest (therapist playing TV star) requires the person answering the question to consult with her (his) team, so that the team approves each answer. Halfway through the game, the *TV Host* introduces the second famous guest.

Therapist as *TV Host:*	And now another famous person who was sexually abused will speak briefly to us and ask some of the questions. She has also talked to magazines, newspapers, and TV shows about being sexually abused as a child. This is a famous beauty queen, who was once Miss America. Would you like to say a few words?
Therapist as Famous *Beauty Queen:*	Yes. I talked about my own sexual abuse because I thought it might help other people know that even someone who was a famous beauty queen might have been sexually abused as a child like I was. I was abused by my father, and I never told anybody about it until I was grown, but it was always something that I worried about in the back of my mind. When I was married and had my own daughter, I got help from therapy, and now I have a successful company of my own, and a very good life and wonderful family. Now let me go on and ask the teams some more of these questions.

The therapist as *TV Host/Emcee* has kept a record of correct team answers, helping teams who appeared to have difficulty with their questions. At the end of the contest, each team is congratulated by the famous hostesses, and each team wins a small treat, such as a Tootsie Roll pop, in addition to the usual refreshments.

3. *Relaxation Practice.*
4. *Cheer* (Ask members to repeat their favorites).

Steps 5 through 8. Same as previous sessions.

Chapter 10 - Groups for Children Ages 6 to 9 and 10 to 12

SESSIONS FIFTEEN AND SIXTEEN

Purpose

To provide closure, reinforce self-esteem, provide transition objects or activities, administer post-test, and celebrate graduation.

Materials Needed

Posttest and pencils, refreshments, small gifts or "transition objects," graduation certificates, Polaroid camera and film, packets or folders of completed coloring book pages, homework, and other written activities, stapled together, one for each member.

Format

1. Role selection.
2. Session tasks: posttesting, graduation, description of therapists' follow-up.
3. Summarization, presentation of small gifts.
4. Cheers and chants.
5. Refreshments.
6. Clean-up.
7. Positive feedback good-byes.

Contents of Sessions Fifteen and Sixteen

It is possible that more sessions should be considered if children were unable to complete the activities described in this chapter. There should be ample time in the last session, however, to complete posttesting and allow time for a joyful "graduation" celebration.

1. *Role Selection.*
2. *Session Task: Graduation.* This is more fun for children if the "ceremony" can be attended by parents/caretakers or a close relative, and if it is as formal as possible. We bring a small tape recorder, play "formal" music, and have each child come forward to receive her (his) certificate. As she (he) receives the certificate, the therapist lists three accomplishments for each child (e.g., always attempted every activity, tried to assist others, always attempted homework, gave lots of good group comments, etc.). The "Graduation Certificates" are included with the supplementary materials in Part IV.
3. *Summarization/Presentation of Small Gifts.* If funds are available, a small transitional object is given to each child after she (he) receives her (his) certificate. The transition object reminds members of their mastery experiences in the group. In our sessions we have given "Beanie Babies" or other stuffed animals, or small, inexpensive sterling silver bracelets purchased from a supportive local merchant. The use of these transitional objects is explained in the following manner: "We want you to always remember what you have learned and how strong you got in this group. So this _(Beanie Baby/bracelet)_ is yours to touch when you feel sad or when you are remembering some of the bad feelings from the past. Or you can touch your _(Beanie Baby/ bracelet)_ when you want to remember the good times we had in this group. You can touch it

and say to yourself, 'That was then, but this is now. I won't be abused, and I know how.' Then you can say, 'I'm a good person, I'm proud of me, I've been through a lot, but look how strong I've got.' Okay let's all practice doing that."

4. *Cheers and Chants.* To end the session, these cheers should be enjoyed. "Let's say them out loud, as loud as we can together while we hold hands."

5. *Refreshments.* These might be extra special for the last session.

6. *Clean-Up.*

7. *Positive Feedback Good-Byes.* Each child should leave the session with more verbal positive stroking good-byes from the therapists. Individual Polaroid photos are wonderful mementos, and each child should also receive her (his) folder of completed activities.

> ***Please Note:*** For the benefit of therapists, parents/caretakers, and group members, it is important to carry out the follow-up activities described in Part II of this book. Be sure to review Chapter 8 before conducting your final group session.

CHAPTER 11

Guide to Supplemental Material for Children's Groups Ages 6 to 12

> The following is a listing of the materials that can be found in Part IV.

THEMES IN THE COLORING BOOK

Pages	Themes
A1	Cover
A3	Sometimes bad things happen despite our efforts.
A4	What we can do about it to take care of ourselves.
A5	Sometimes adults do bad things to children.
A6	What we can do about it: learn about it, say no, talk to others, learn about our feelings, and be a member of a group.
A7	About abusers: They have problems.
A8	What we can do about it: understanding, telling, and calling 911.
A9	Sexual abuse can happen to children no matter how good they are.
A10	It is never the child's fault.
A11	Good secrets and bad secrets: how abusers try to keep their abuse secret.
A12	Learning the difference between good and bad secrets, not keeping bad secrets.
A13	We might not always feel safe.
A14	What we can do about it: learning who is a safe person and who is not.
A15	Why parents/caretakers can't tell that their children are being abused; children have to tell.
A16	Children must learn to tell.
A17	When abusers threaten children, children still must learn to tell.
A18	What happens when you tell, and what happens if you don't tell; TELL!
A19	Confused feelings about the abuser and good and bad touches.
A20	Learning about the confused feelings; despite confusion, your body is all your own and no one has the right to touch it.
A21	After you tell, you might still have some bad feelings you have to learn how to handle.
A22	Learning about the feelings and talking to yourself.
A23	What happens to the abuser; abusers need special help.
A24	You are not guilty for telling or for causing the abuser to go to jail. You have a right to tell.
A25	We don't know how to cure people from abusing children.
A26	Sometimes abusers are cured if they get help, but it is more important for the child to be safe; sexual abuse is against the law and never the child's fault.

A27   Sometimes children have bad dreams or angry feelings even after the abuse stops.
A28   Children can learn how to handle their feelings about being abused.
A29   Children who have been abused can learn to feel good about themselves and grow up to be happy.

COMMENTS AND THEMES
REGARDING THE HOMEWORK ASSIGNMENTS

Assignments	Pages	Themes
#1	D3	Assigned in Session Two, reviewed in Session Three: Facts about sexual abuse: definitions of good and bad touches, our bodies are private, I am not the only one that abuse happened to, it is not my fault (coordinates with material on coloring book page A6)
#2	D4	Assigned in Session Three, reviewed in Session Four: Abusers are wrong, and children can learn how to get the abuse stopped, how to talk to other adults about it (coordinates with material on coloring book page A8).
#3	D5-D6	Assigned in Session Four, reviewed in Session Five: Good and bad secrets, safe and unsafe people, code words for safety (coordinates with coloring book pages A12 and A14).
#4	D7	Assigned in Session Five, reviewed in Session Six: Review of material in Sessions One through Four (coordinates with material on coloring book pages A15-A18).
#5	D8-D9	Assigned in Session Six, reviewed in Session Seven: Why it is hard to tell about abuse, why mothers/caretakers don't always know their children are being abused, mothers/caretakers always want their children to be safe (coordinates with *Wanda's Story*, pp. D13-D16, and review coloring book pages A15-A18).
#6	D10	Assigned in Session Seven, reviewed in Session Eight: A review of why some adults abuse children; children have a right to be safe from abusers (coordinates with *My Own Story*, pp. D17-D18, and also pages A7-A8 and A23-A26 in coloring book).
#7	D11-D12	Assigned in Session Eight, reviewed in Session Nine: Confused feelings about abuse even after the child tells, what to do about the feelings (coordinates with coloring book pages A19-A20, and also see pages A21-A23).

ADDITIONAL ITEMS

Pages	Items
B1-B6	*Feeling Faces* (use with Sessions Four, Six, and Seven).
C1-C8	*"Draw-A-Picture" Sheets* (use with Session Four).
E1-E5 and J3-J8	*Moving On and Getting Stronger Game* and Learning Cards (use for Sessions Twelve and Fourteen)
F1-F4	Graduation Certificates (use with Sessions Fifteen and Sixteen).

Groups for Sexually Abused Teens Ages 13 to 16

In order to avoid redundancy, we note here that the group content for older members is similar to that of younger groups, and that much of the preceding material applies. In working with teens, however, we also emphasize peer assistance and confrontation, miniature real-life situations, and human relations skills in ways that allow for their typical swings between rebellion and submission. In our work with sexually abused teens we have attempted to infuse the groups with a sense of protection from the adult world while at the same time challenging their feelings of differentness and isolation.

SESSION ONE

Purpose

To familiarize members with group format, alleviate anxiety, build expectations for participation and behavior, and initiate cognitive relabeling and desensitization.

Materials Needed

Provided it has not already been administered, the Pretest (Form GM, p. 37), The "Worry List" (p. 40), answer sheets (one per member, pp. 38-39 and 41), pens or pencils, clipboards, foam ball (optional), and tape player and prerecorded tape (also optional).

Format

1. Therapists' introduction/discussion.
2. Pretesting.
3. Group introductions and "Name Game."
4. "Cheers and Chants" for positive self-concept and cognitive behavior modification.
5. Refreshments for social skills and nurturing.
6. Clean-up for closure.
7. Positive reinforcement good-byes by therapists.

Contents of Session One

1. *Therapists' Introduction/Discussion.* The therapists introduce themselves, defining the purpose of the group as one that will help members deal with their feelings about sexual abuse, learn the facts and myths about sexual abuse, and find ways to be stronger and safe from abuse. "You know that everyone in this group has been abused, and that many people think that one in every five girls in the United States has been sexually abused. In addition to the general goals we have talked about, we are going to work on some specific goals and rules for our group. But first we have to get to know each other a little bit and have you take a short test — not like a school test, just your opinion about things."

2. *Administration of Pretest.* This can be read aloud by therapist or given to each member, with a clipboard, to complete on her (his) own.

3. *Acquainting Members with One Another:* (a) Divide the group into pairs (uneven numbers will pair with a group therapist). Direct the pairs into corners of the room to learn enough about each other so that they can come back into the group and "introduce" their partners. Questions for each member to ask her (his) partner include name, age, school and grade, what she (he) does in her (his) spare time, what she (he) thinks she (he) would like to do when she (he) is out of school, the person she (he) would most like to be like and why, what she (he) thinks is the best and worst thing about herself (himself), and who sexually abused her (him).

   After each set of partners has been introduced, proceed to (b) (name familiarity). See the Critter "Name Game" in Chapter 10, which describes linking each member's first name with a critter with the same first letter (Patsy Parrot, Tina Tiger, Phyllis Panda, etc.). Have each member go around the group listing all the names and critters in order, or throw a foam ball randomly around the group while each person says her (his) own name and critter along with name and critter of the person to whom she (he) throws the ball.

   (c) Another name exercise to try is to have each member choose an "action" or dancelike movement. The whole group stands up and, in synchronization with pop music from a tape player, goes around performing each person's movement while shouting out her (his) name.

4. *Cheers and Chants* (in the manner described in Chapter 10):

That was THEN but this is NOW.
I won't be ABUSED, and I'll learn HOW!

5. *Refreshments for Social Skills and Nurturing.* Therapists may use this opportunity to explain the role basket and procedure to be followed in next session.

6. *Clean-Up.*

7. *Positive Reinforcement Good-Byes.* Therapists stand at the door, shake each member's hand, and tell what they liked best about what each member did or said in the group. This is important for self-esteem building and for reinforcing behavior changes.

SESSION TWO

Purpose

To promote group cohesion, alleviate anxiety, set expectations for group behavior, practice self-identification as sexually abused, introduce concepts of cognitive restructuring, and practice mastery, assertiveness, social skills, and problem solving.

Materials Needed:

Role selection basket, foam ball for "Name Game," *That Was Then, But This Is Now* booklets (one per member; pp. G1-G18), pencils, clipboards, blackboard/chalk or easel/markers, Homework Assignment #1, and refreshments.

Format

1. "Name Game" (optional, depending on how well names were learned in Session One).
2. Role selection and review of tasks.
3. Session task: *That Was Then, But This Is Now* booklets: My Three Wishes.
4. Chant.
5. Summarization by group summarizer.
6. Refreshments and clean-up.
7. Homework assignment explained and reviewed.
8. Positive feedback good-byes.

Contents of Session Two

1. *Name Practice and Group Introduction Exercises.* It may be helpful to begin this session with another round of the "get acquainted" critter or action games to help form group cohesion and remind members of one another's names.
2. *Role Assignment.* Each member is randomly assigned a role she (he) will take for the session by drawing a card from the role basket. Please see role descriptions in Chapter 10; depending on the session task and the number of group members, cards should include *Hostess (Host), Rules Watcher, Homework Person* (Note: Unlike that for younger groups, the homework for older groups is open-ended, so the *Homework Person* is responsible for checking that homework has been done, collecting it, and initiating its discussion), *Group Helper, Group Actor(s), Group Neatness Officer* (can be combined with rules function), *Reminder* or *Summarizer*, and *Complimenter.*
3. *Session Task.* Each member should be given a small booklet, *That Was Then, But This Is Now* (my own getting safe and strong book) which contains a number of blank pages with headings. Members will complete these pages during the next several sessions, keeping them as a reminder of the goals and process of the group. Therapists will take them up and redistribute them during each session in which they are used. Unlike the younger groups' coloring books, which are best distributed a few pages at a time, *That Was Then, But This Is Now* may be prepared as full booklets in advance of the first session.

Therapist: This is your own booklet, *That Was Then, But This is Now,* my own getting safe and strong book. You will be keeping a record of the goals you set for yourself, the goals and rules the group sets for everyone, and some reminders about the activities and things we talk about in the group, so you will remember them after the group is finished. The first activity is for each of you to complete the first page, "My Three Wishes." List three things you wish had been different in your life, related to the sexual abuse.

When members have finished writing, make a list of all the wishes on the blackboard or on a large sheet of paper. The following is a list of the most common wishes of our group members. I wish that:

✓ the abuse never had happened
✓ the sexual abuse had not been by someone like a parent or stepparent that I liked and trusted
✓ it would never happen again
✓ it would never happen to my sisters or brothers — or anyone
✓ the abuse had not been more than just once
✓ I could just forget about it
✓ the person who did it would not deny it
✓ my parent/caretaker and everyone else had believed me from the beginning
✓ I could understand why someone would do this to me
✓ I had known not to trust some people, and knew whom I could trust
✓ I could have been able to have sex for the first time with someone I really loved
✓ the person who did it could be cured
✓ if he (she) could be cured, that our family could be back together again

Writing out these wishes always includes extended discussion in the groups, allowing for a cathartic, accepting exploration of feelings about the abuse experience. Following their listing and discussion, the wishes are used to explain and develop the group's goals, which can also be listed on paper or chalkboard. Members are told, "In some ways we can work on making parts of these wishes come true. Let's write down which parts of these wishes we can work on." Using the examples above, the cognitive restructuring needed to transform wishes into goals might be described in the following manner:

Wish #1. We cannot magically go back and have the abuse disappear. But we will learn to handle feelings and fears about the sexual abuse. You will learn how to handle feelings not only about the sexual abuse, but about other difficult things that happen in your life and make you a stronger person who feels good about taking care of herself (himself). And we can learn how to get help from other people when we really need it.

Wish #2. We will learn that it can be normal to have two opposite feelings about the same people, and that people who have many good things about them can also have a sick, opposite side which results in their sexually abusing others. In fact, many people who sexually abuse children are deliberately extra nice to them at other times so the children will feel confused and hesitate to tell about the abuse.

Wish #3. We can definitely learn to make ourselves safer, and most people can learn how to keep from being abused again. We can all learn ways to keep from being a victim, not only of sexual abuse, but also in other parts of our lives. We can learn where to go for help and how to ask for it.

Wish #4. We will learn ways to teach our own children and brothers and sisters to recognize sexual abuse, how they can try to keep themselves safe, and where to go for help.

Wish #5. We can learn that most people have fears and worries about telling about the abuse, so it usually happens more than once. But when you understand the reasons people are fearful or worried about whether to tell, you will understand that you probably did the best you could at the time, and that you don't need to feel guilty or surprised that it happened more than once.

Wish #6. In some ways it is not good to completely forget anything that has happened to us, even though we would like to at times. At least we can learn from the sexual abuse how to take care of ourselves, how to get help from others, and whom to trust. And the sad and scary thoughts about sexual abuse can be changed a lot. We can learn about "thought stopping" when the thoughts get too frightening or sad, and we can learn to change around some of the ways we think about the abuse. Instead of thinking, "It's so sad that I was sexually abused, I feel awful," we learn to say to ourselves, "It is sad that I didn't know what I know now. But I am a good person, and I have gotten stronger because of what I know about taking care of myself. I don't have to be a victim." We will learn to say, "I'm a good person, I'm proud of me. I've been through a lot, but look how strong I've got!"

Wish #7. It would be nice if we could make the abuser confess in front of everyone. But sometimes sexual abusers are too afraid, or feel too guilty to ever admit what they have done. What we *can* do is practice what we'd like to say to them and learn about why they can't admit the abuse.

Wish #8. We can learn all the fears and feelings that a parent/caretaker has about their child being sexually abused. We can learn that it is usually so frightening and makes parents/caretakers so angry that their children have been abused, that they almost cannot let themselves believe it. Sometimes it is so upsetting that they try to convince themselves that it cannot be true, that this could not be happening right in their own families. This makes it easier to understand why your parents/caretakers had trouble believing you, and makes it easier for you to forgive them.

Wish #9. Although we never know exactly what causes a certain abuser to sexually abuse a child, we know in general that people who do this are sick in their minds, even if they look healthy and normal on the outside. We learn that it has nothing to do with anything you did, but with the sickness, problems, and willingness of the abusers to ignore the law and what they knew was harmful for a child.

Wish #10. Unless you had been in a group like this, there is probably no way you could have known which people you could trust. In fact, you are usually taught to trust all the adults you know, and would not expect them to abuse you. In this group we are going to learn about situations we can avoid, what to do when these things happen, and how to handle situations where people we thought we could trust become sexually abusive.

Wish #11. In this group, we will learn that sexual abuse is not the same as grown-up loving sex between two people who really care about each other and are ready for the responsibilities of a grown-up, loving sexual relationship. What has happened to you is not that kind of sex, which you will have with your husband (wife) when you grow up. Sexual abuse, which was done just for the sake of the abuser, was not your fault.

Wish #12. There are some programs which seem to help sexual abusers, and we will talk about some of the methods they use. But people have to be willing to go to the programs and truly work on changing themselves. This is hard to do, and many sexual abusers are not willing to do it. In the end it is usually best to accept that it is very hard for an abuser to change, that most of them are not willing to work as hard as it takes to change, and that you cannot trust them not to abuse someone else again.

Wish #13. Sometimes families are able to get back together, and sometimes sexual abusers are willing to work very hard and make changes in themselves. But we have to learn that this is rare and very difficult. If your family is going to be back together again with the person who sexually abused you, there have to be some very definite rules about how you can be kept safe in that family. And you have to know how to get help if these rules are not kept.

4. *Chant for Second Session, Used for Cognitive Relabeling, Self-Esteem Building, and Group Cohesion:*

My BODY is PRIVATE, it BELONGS to ME.
NOBODY has a RIGHT to my BODY but ME.
It's NOT my FAULT that I was ABUSED,
But the ONE who ABUSED me should NOT be EXCUSED.

5. *Summarization.* The group member assigned the role of *Summarizer*, with the assistance of therapists, verbalizes the goals of the session, the tasks of the session, what she (he) learned, what she (he) liked best about the session, and any incomplete work she (he) would like to have extended into the next session.
6. *Refreshments and Clean-Up.*
7. *Homework Assignments Are Distributed.* Instructions are to complete the task with parents or caretakers. Please refer to Chapter 10, Session Two.
8. *Positive Feedback Good-Byes.*

SESSION THREE

Purpose:

To enhance good parent-child relations, provide opportunities for catharsis and restructuring, to establish group rules, to receive input on didactic materials, and to acquaint the group with basic facts about sexual abuse.

Materials Needed:

Role basket, *That Was Then, But This Is Now* booklets, stapled copies of *"Wouldn't It Be Nice"* booklets, pencils, clipboards, chalkboard/chalk or easel/markers, *The Life Game* (optional), Homework Assignment #2, and refreshments.

Format:

1. "Name Game" (optional, depending on how well names were learned in Sessions One and Two).
2. Role selection.
3. Homework discussion and review.
4. Session task: *That Was Then, But This Is Now* booklets: Three Things I Need Band-Aids For.
5. Development of group rules.
6. Review of materials used for younger groups.
7. Cheer.
8. Summarization by group summarizer.
9. Refreshments and clean-up.
10. Homework.
11. Positive feedback good-byes.

Contents of Session Three

Because the remaining groups adhere to the same format, in the following sections we describe session tasks, cheers, and other contents only as they differ from session to session.

Steps 1 to 3. As described previously.

4. *Session Task.* The focus for this session, which may include parents and caretakers, is on the "hurts" that group members have experienced. These are listed in the members' booklets on the "Band-Aid page," written on the blackboard, and then cognitively restructured into goals for the group. Below are some typical examples from our members' lists of "Things that hurt me that I need a Band-Aid for:"

   - the way things changed with my parent/caretaker, and my parent/caretaker not believing me about the abuse

- angry feelings: in addition to angry feelings about the abuse and toward the abuser, angry feelings toward my parent/caretaker (because I thought she [he] did not believe me, or I thought she [he] should have known about the abuse and stopped it)
- not understanding why my parent/caretaker didn't realize the abuse was going on and why she (he) didn't stop it
- losing somebody I cared about, and the family losing him (her) because of the abuse (father [wife], stepfather [stepmother], etc.)
- other people in the family making me feel left out or that the abuse must have been my fault
- feeling that I am different, inside and outside, from other people my age, and feeling that other people can tell I have been abused
- feeling very confused, and that I don't really understand why the abuse happened, and what was going on in my family during the abuse and afterward

When parents/caretakers attend these sessions, they are encouraged to make a "Hurt and Band-Aid Need" list of their own to be written out on the board and discussed in the group. The most common "hurts" listed by parents/caretakers have been:

- feelings of hurt and betrayal toward the abuser who was often a husband (wife) or boyfriend (girlfriend)
- mixed feelings of needing support and help for the family from the abuser, toward whom they also feel disgust and anger
- concern that instead of being closer, mother-daughter (father-son) relations are more difficult to handle, and just at the time when parents/caretakers, despite their own confused, angry feelings toward the abuser, have more responsibility and concerns for the whole family
- believing that everyone — family, social services, schools, and therapists — is critical of them for not being more protective of their daughters (sons).

These "hurts" are then rewritten as goals for the group in the same manner shown for Session Two. Writing the goals provides opportunities for cathartic discussion of the hurts as well as suggestions for changing the ways these situations are viewed and dealt with.

5. *Development of Group Rules.* After using the "hurts" to develop a list of the group's general goals, members should work on a brief list of group "rules" to be monitored by the *Rules Enforcer* (role chosen from the role basket). Typical rules chosen by members and therapists have been:

- Not being late for group, and letting us know when you can't come and why.
- Everybody has to try each exercise, and do the best she (he) can with it.
- Everybody should get a chance to talk and not be interrupted.
- No cursing or calling each other names.
- No talking about what goes on in the group to other people (other than parents when homework is discussed).

6. Review of *"Wouldn't It Be Nice"* coloring books used by younger children. These are distributed to group members, introduced by therapists as materials with which members may want to

help their younger siblings understand sexual abuse. Therapists may also request input concerning the coloring book format: "If you were younger when the sexual abuse happened, do you think these would have helped you? What else do you think we should put in them?" Reviewing the coloring book serves two purposes: to actually receive input into development of materials, and to acquaint members with basic facts about sexual abuse in very simple terms.

Members are asked to write in their *That Was Then, But This Is Now* booklets on the page for "Things I Would Like to See Added to the *'Wouldn't It Be Nice'* Coloring Book." Therapists may explain this task in the following manner: "This is where you can write down the things that are not talked about in the coloring book which older kids and teens need to know about. They can be anything you would like to know about, understand, and talk about in the group that's not covered in the younger kids' coloring book."

Subjects about which teenagers have requested information include venereal disease, concerns about birth control (for girls: especially why they didn't become pregnant from the abuse), and the truth about lies and myths they were told by abusers (e.g., that rubbing breasts makes them bigger; that once you have had sex, you can't help wanting it; that boys [girls] can tell you have had sex and will only want you for one thing; etc.).

Often teens will express concerns about developmental issues which are unrelated to the abuse and represent needs for social skills development. In addition to information about sexual abuse, many of these issues are presented in an interesting and therapeutic fashion through the group's use of *The Life Game*, developed by this author and included in Part IV.

If time permits, *The Life Game* can be demonstrated or even played; therapists may wish simply to refer to it as a way group members will be learning the answers to some of their questions in future sessions.

7. *Group Cheer* (use cheer from Session Two):

My BODY is PRIVATE, it BELONGS to ME.
NOBODY has a RIGHT to my BODY but ME.
It's NOT my FAULT that I was ABUSED,
But the ONE who ABUSED me should NOT be EXCUSED.

8. *Homework Assignment #2.*

Steps 9 through 11. Same as previous sessions.

SESSION FOUR

Purpose:

To review facts/myths about sexual abuse and to provide further opportunities for cognitive restructuring.

Materials Needed:

Role basket, *The Life Game*, throwing die, playing pieces (one per member), Homework Assignment #3, and refreshments.

Format:

1. Role selection.
2. Session task: *The Life Game*.
3. Group cheer.
4. Summarization.
5. Refreshments and clean-up.
6. Homework assignment.
7. Positive feedback good-byes.

Contents of Session Four

Step 1. As previously described.

2. *Session Task: Reviewing Facts and Myths about Sexual Abuse by Playing* The Life Game (pp. I1-J28). In this game, each member throws a die and moves a corresponding number of spaces on the game board, answering a Learning Card each time she (he) throws a one or a two. (See game description on pp. I1-I2 for complete instructions.) Learning Cards are designed to stimulate discussion of some aspect of sexual abuse. Depending on the needs of the group, therapists may also use Problem-Solving, Knowing Yourself, and Understanding Each Other cards to stimulate discussion about typical teen concerns and issues. The primary use of the game in this session, however, is to learn about sexual abuse.

    This is a session which parents or caretakers may attend. They may wish to join the discussion and be included in *The Life Game*. If adults do join the game, they should be instructed to answer the questions first as they would have done as teens, and then to answer as they would now.

    Some of the myths about sexual abuse (and corresponding responses therapists should make) are that:

    Myth: Girls bring sexual abuse on themselves by acting or dressing "too sexy."
    Fact: We know that this is not true, and that the abuse is the fault of the abuser, who has special kinds of problems that make him (her) want to have sex with very young people. It has nothing to do with the way you dressed or acted. Sometimes abusers say this to you to make you feel guilty and afraid to tell about the abuse.

Myth: Fathers (mothers) and other family members have some rights to use your body.

Fact: Nobody has any rights to your body but you. Men (Women) who say these things are sick or selfish, with special problems. They know this is not true. They just say these kinds of things to try to get you to go along with the abuse.

Myth: Sexual abuse is not all bad, because it will teach you about sex.

Fact: Sexual abuse does not teach you about what sex is really like when you are old enough to understand a loving, responsible, sexual relationship between two adults. Sexual abuse comes at a time when your mind and body are not ready for sexuality, and abusers are just using their victims for their own pleasure even though they know that what they are doing is wrong and against the law. You will learn that adults who are normal turn their sexual feelings toward other adults in a caring, legal way, and do not turn their sexual feelings towards children.

Myth: Everything that is connected with the sexual abuser and the sexual abuse is always awful and hurtful.

Fact: The sexual abuse is hurtful because you are not ready for this, because it is confusing and upsetting, and because the sexual abuser knows that this is harmful for you. But *everything* about the abuse is not always unpleasant. The abuser often tries to do many good things for you, such as buying things for you, taking you special places, and so on, so that you will like him (her) and not tell about the abuse. Sometimes the abuse starts off in a pleasant way with many hugs, perhaps some kisses that seem okay, and then usually progresses to actions that are confusing and upsetting — more sexual kinds of things that you are asked to do, or things that are done to you.

Myth: A parent/caretaker really knows what is happening, and should stop the abuse; if she (he) were a good parent/caretaker, she (he) would know even if no one told her (him).

Fact: No parent/caretaker wants her (his) child to be sexually abused. And it is a very hard thing to realize that someone she (he) trusted would do such a thing. Also the abusers are often very good liars and know how to hide what they are doing. Many parents/caretakers say that they might have guessed what was going on, but it was just too hard for them to believe that such a thing could happen in their homes. They often dread even having such a suspicion, because it hurts so much to think it could happen.

Myth: If a parent/caretaker really loved you, she (he) would never have anything to do with the person who abused you after she (he) learned about the abuse, and she (he) would never have any feelings but anger and hatred toward the abuser.

Fact: Abusers often have some good things about them. They can be very nice sometimes, and very helpful. They can take good care of their families in some ways. So a parent/caretaker often has some of the same confused feelings that her (his) child does: she (he) hates the abuse, but can't forget many of the good things that the abuser has done for the family. Sometimes parents/caretakers believe that the abuse is a sickness or mental problem that they should help abusers get treatment for. That is true, but they should also know that it is *very difficult* to cure people who sexually abuse others, and the probability is strong that a sexual abuser will continue to abuse others, even if he (she) is willing to get some treatment.

Myth: A sexually abused child or adolescent is a damaged person who will never get over the abuse.

Fact: Being sexually abused is a difficult and sad thing to happen to people. But people do get past it and learn to handle their feelings and go on with their lives. They learn a lot in therapy or group sessions like ours, talk with their friends, read about abuse, and learn special ways to cope with their feelings, as we will do. Some very famous and successful people have talked about overcoming sexual abuse, including a famous TV star as well as a famous beauty queen.

Myth: No boyfriend (girlfriend) or husband (wife) will understand about the sexual abuse, and he (she) will hold it against you.

Fact: Most mature, understanding husbands (wives) and boyfriends (girlfriends) will understand about the abuse. They will not hold it against you, because most people understand that abuse is not the child's fault, but the fault of the abuser. You can learn to feel good about yourself, and know that other people will understand.

Myth: Children and teens can't really do anything to stop the abuse, and they are powerless to keep it from happening again.

Fact: Children and teens can learn that there are ways to get help to keep from being sexually abused. They can learn where to go for help and how to say that they need help. Because sexual abuse is against the law, they can involve the police and social services who will help them. That is one of the reasons for this group: to learn that other people do not have power over you to sexually abuse you. Now that you know what to do and whom to ask for help, you do not have to be abused again.

Myth: You will never be able to get over your bad feelings about being abused.

Fact: With some help, such as this group or a counselor, you can learn many ways of handling your bad feelings about being abused. Everybody has some bad things happen in life, and we all have to learn how to handle our feelings about them and to get on with the things we want to do to make ourselves happy.

If parents or caretakers are involved in this session, they may also wish to bring up some myths or mistaken ideas they have heard about sexual abuse. Ask group members to share any other "myths" they have heard.

3. *Group Cheer* (use cheer from Session Two):

> My BODY is PRIVATE, it BELONGS to ME.
> NOBODY has a RIGHT to my BODY but ME.
> It's NOT my FAULT that I was ABUSED,
> But the ONE who ABUSED me should NOT be EXCUSED.

Steps 4 through 7. As previously described.

Chapter 12 - Groups for Sexually Abused Teens Ages 13 to 16

SESSION FIVE

Purpose:

To build self-esteem and to provide opportunities for cognitive restructuring and desensitization.

Materials Needed:

Role basket, *The Life Game*, *That Was Then, But This Is Now* booklets, mirror, pencils, clipboards, Homework Assignment #4, and refreshments.

Format:

1. Role selection.
2. Homework review.
3. Session task: Mirror, Mirror, On the Wall and *The Life Game*.
4. Group cheer.
5. Summarization.
6. Refreshments and clean-up.
7. Homework assignment.
8. Positive feedback good-byes.

Contents of Session Five

Steps 1 to 2. As previously discussed.

3. *Session Task: Mirror, Mirror on the Wall.* Using the instructions and questions listed in Chapter 10, Session Eleven, each member is asked to use a mirror to ask any question she (he) has about sexual abuse, herself (himself), or any ideas she (he) may think has not been covered by the group. If members are unable to produce questions spontaneously, some have been suggested in Chapter 10 for the therapist to "whisper" to them to use. *That Was Then, But This Is Now* booklets contain pages for members to write down questions they would like to ask the Magic Mirror. (If you have additional time, feel free to play *The Life Game*.)

4. *Group Cheer* (in all subsequent sessions: use any chant/cheer from Chapter 10 or from earlier sessions).

Steps 5 through 8. As previously described.

SESSION SIX

Purpose:

To teach self-sufficiency, self-responsibility, and prevention: How to recognize and handle potentially abusive situations.

Materials Needed:

Role basket, Homework Assignment #5, and refreshments.

Format:

1. Role selection.
2. Homework review.
3. Session task: taking care of yourself.
4. Group cheer.
5. Summarization.
6. Refreshments and clean-up.
7. Homework assignment.
8. Positive feedback good-byes.

Contents of Session Six

Steps 1 to 2. As previously described.

3. *Session Task: Taking Care of Yourself Role-Plays.* After role cards have been drawn, group members will take turns playing the following situations. Group members who selected the *Group Actor* cards will play the potential abusers:

Scenario #1: A teacher asks you to stay after class, closes the door, and sits really close to you, looking at your homework, but begins to talk about how pretty you are and how you could get better grades if you would just "cooperate" with him (her).

Scenario #2: An older cousin (male) asks you to go on a little walk at a family picnic, but after you sit down to look at the view, he starts to put his hand on your leg, telling you how grown-up you look, and that you need to learn how to "handle men."

Scenario #3: Your divorced mother's boyfriend asks you to go to the grocery store with him to help with the marketing, but instead of coming right back home, drives to a park and starts talking about how pretty you are, and how you are prettier than your mother, and moves over very close to you.

Scenario #4: You are left with an older uncle while your aunt has gone next door. He starts talking about how grown-up you are, and how you need to know about sex and men's bodies so you can handle yourself, and acts as if he might unzip his pants.

Scenario #5:   You are at a movie, and leave to get some popcorn. There is nobody in the lobby, and the cute youngish guy (girl) working there says he (she) needs to get some change in the office, and asks if you will come with him (her).

Scenario #6:   A nice looking man (woman) you don't know calls you over to his (her) car and asks where a certain address is. There is a lady (man) in the backseat. They say they don't understand how to get there, and ask if you will go with them, just down the street to find the address.

Scenario #7:   A woman (man) you and your family don't know very well is hired to stay with you and your younger brothers and sisters while your parents go out for a special evening. The woman (man) has a book with her (him) that she (he) says has pictures you need to see and learn about so you will understand about your body parts. She (he) wants you to show your private body parts to see if they match the pictures.

Scenario #8:   Your mother has been very sick for a long time, and your father calls you into his bedroom and says that you should have sex with him, because your mother is too sick, and otherwise he will have to leave the family and find another woman for sex, and that would, "just kill your mother."

Scenario #9:   Your older brother (sister) tells you that he (she) will take you some places with some really cute friends of his (hers), but you have to know all about sex and stuff so you will not seem dumb. He (She) wants to "teach" you some things about sex, and tries to come into your bedroom one night when your parents are out at a movie.

Scenario #10:   A camp counselor (or scout leader) who has seemed very nice, sees you alone, and wants to show you some pictures of people having sex. She (He) says that you should know about these things, so that you will know about the different kinds of sex there are, and later you can choose which you really would like.

Therapists should present as many role-playing scenarios as time allows. The more repeated opportunities members have to practice saying "No," dialing 911, and "telling," the better prepared they are to recognize and avoid potential sexual abuse.

Steps 4 through 8. As previously described.

SESSION SEVEN

Purpose:

To provide catharsis and provide opportunities to process feelings, to enhance self-esteem, and to promote relabeling.

Materials Needed:

Role basket, blank booklets (one for each member to be used to take notes or write down special or important things), pencils, clipboards, Homework Assignment #6, and refreshments.

Format:

1. Role selection.
2. Homework review.
3. Session tasks: Letter to the Abuser; The 21-Year-Old Visit to the Abuser.
4. Group cheer.
5. Summarization.
6. Refreshments and clean-up.
7. Homework assignment.
8. Positive feedback good-byes.

Contents of Session Seven

Steps 1 to 2. As previously described.

3. *Session Tasks:* (a) *Letter to the Abuser.* Group members are asked to write a cooperative letter that could be sent to any or all of their abusers. The therapists tell them that even though they certainly do not have to mail the letter, the purpose of the exercise is to help decide what they would really like to say. Each member can add specifics about her (his) own situation. The therapist writes out the letter and has copies made during the session so that each member may put the letter in her (his) booklet. If a group member demonstrates a strong desire to actually mail her (his) letter, therapists should initiate a discussion of the consequences of doing so, requesting that the member consider the consequences with her (his) parent/caretaker before she (he) actually mails the letter. Members should understand that the purpose of the letter is for cathartic expression of feelings, rather than actual contact with the abuser, which may have negative effects.

    Therapists may explain these negative consequences by saying something like, "An abuser can often confuse things in his or her own mind, and this is one reason he or she is a sexual abuser. He or she may think in his or her mind that you want to contact him or her so that the abuse can begin again, no matter what you say in the letter. He or she may use it to defend himself or herself by telling even more lies about the abuse to your family or other people."

    (b) *The 21-Year-Old Visit.* Therapists instruct members to envision themselves at 21 years old: possessing a wonderful job, beautiful car, lots of nice clothes, and full awareness that they are grown and that their abusers cannot hurt them. Members imagine themselves arriving at the abusers' homes or offices, and rehearse what they would like to say to them.

Many teens feel that they never want to have any contact with their abusers, and indicate that they never want to visit or see them in any way. These members should be assured that this way of handling their feelings is fine; however, that this exercise is not a "plan" but an imaginary situation where they would be safe and nothing bad could happen. "In a situation like that," the therapist asks, "what would you like to say and do to the person who abused you?"

At the end of this visualization members are reminded that there are always consequences to everything we do, but that when they are adults, there is little an abuser will be able to do to hurt them. Discuss the positive and negative consequences of such a visit if it were real.

Steps 4 through 8. As previously described.

SESSION EIGHT

Purpose:

To enhance self-esteem, relabeling, and acknowledgment/awareness of feelings and to stimulate optimism about the future.

Materials Needed:

Role basket, blank booklets, clipboards, pencils, Homework Assignment #7, and refreshments.

Format:

1. Role selection.
2. Homework review.
3. Session tasks: What's Good About Me, What Abuse Made Me Feel, and What I Can Expect to Change About Me.
4. Group cheer.
5. Summarization.
6. Refreshments and clean-up.
7. Homework assignment.
8. Positive feedback good-byes.

Contents of Session Eight

Steps 1 to 2. As previously described.

3. *Session Tasks:* (a) *What's Good About Me.* This is a helpful session for mothers/caretakers to attend. Members are asked to list 10 good things about themselves in their booklets. Therapists explain, "These 10 good things about yourself can be something you have done that was good, or something that you like about yourself, or something others have said they liked." Sometimes members need assistance from one another and from therapists. Everyone's list should be read aloud.

   (b) *What Abuse Made Me Feel.* Next, members are instructed to list in their booklets three ways that they believe the abuse made them feel badly about themselves.

   (c) *What I Can Expect to Change About Me.* Below the list of three bad feelings on the workbook page, members write down what they have learned in the group that will help them deal with their feelings, and how they can expect to feel next year, and in 3 years. Positive but realistic expectations should be encouraged.

Steps 4 through 8. Same as previous sessions.

SESSION NINE

Purpose:

To teach negotiation principles and skills, practice negotiation skills, enhance self-esteem, and provide further relabeling opportunities.

Materials Needed:

Role basket, blank booklets, chalkboard/chalk or easel/markers, pencils, clipboards, large sheet of paper, Homework Assignment #8, and refreshments.

Format:

1. Role selection.
2. Homework review.
3. Session task: Learning negotiation skills.
4. Group cheer.
5. Summarization.
6. Refreshments and clean-up.
7. Homework assignment.
8. Positive feedback good-byes.

Contents of Session Nine

Steps 1 to 2. As previously described.

3. *Session Task: Negotiation Practice – How to Get What You Want in a Good Way.* A shortened version of the rules for negotiation are listed in the *That Was Then, But This Is Now* booklets; however, these should be discussed, reviewed, and written on a blackboard or large sheet of paper. (Instruct group members to write these rules down in their booklet.) The following discussion provides some suggestions.

Rules for Negotiation

1. Know exactly what actions you want from the other person or specifically what you would like him or her to do.
2. Be able to communicate those actions to the other person in a clear, polite manner.
3. Be able to give clear, adequate reasons WHY you want or need something from the other person.
4. Suggest some solutions to any problems you expect the person might have in doing this for you.
5. Explain and apologize for any misunderstanding or confusion in the past that has prevented this person from doing what you are asking of him or her.
6. Offer something to the other person in return for his or her cooperation.
7. Be ready to suggest some compromise or an alternative solution.
8. Express appreciation for any change or compromise from the other person.

Before role-playing exercises begin, it is helpful for therapists to give examples of the preceding steps, using a common conflict between parents and teens such as privacy in their rooms. An example might resemble the following:

Step 1   (what actions are wanted): Parent/Caretaker not to come into bedroom and go through teen's clothing or purse, or read her/his mail, and so forth.

Steps 2 and 3   (communicate clearly, politely, give clear reasons why you want something): "Mom, it really makes me feel bad that I have no place that is my own. I don't feel like I have any privacy, and you know that you have your own rules about your privacy. What I would like is if you would not come in my room or go through my things without asking me. I would really appreciate your trying to do this for me and it would mean a lot."

Step 4   (suggest solutions): "I know that in the past you said that you had to go in my room to clean it up and make it look decent. What I want to do is to clean it up myself so you won't have to go in there. Then you could go in with me once a week and we could look at things together and you could check that I'm keeping it straightened up. It may not be as clean as you'd keep it, but you could see it's picked up and you wouldn't have to go in there and go through my stuff."

Step 5   (explain and apologize for problems in the past): "I know I was careless in the past with my stuff, and even brought some pot home once. But you know I've never done that again, and I promise not to bring anything home that you'd object to, and promise to keep my room pretty straight if you'll do this for me."

Step 6   (offer something in return): "If you'll do this for me, (it will save you the work of cleaning my room *or* I'll do the dishes every weekend *or* I'll wash your car every weekend" *or* any chore that you think would be a motivating reason for parent/caretaker to go along with your request).

Step 7   (be ready to suggest a compromise if the other person won't give what you want): "Okay, why can't we just try this for 1 week. Then if I can't keep up my end of the bargain, you can go through my room and I won't say anything."

Step 8   (express appreciation): "Thanks for listening, _____. You really try to understand what I need and try to be fair, even though it is hard. I really appreciate it."

Following this discussion, the session's *Group Actors* and other members will practice negotiation situations. A few practice sessions such as those below, where group members take roles of parents and teens, should be followed by real conflict situations suggested by members.

Therapists act as coaches, helping with roles and referring members to each step of the negotiation process. As the role-playing progresses, therapists should request suggestions from other members. The following negotiation scenarios are offered as warm-ups:

Scenario #1:   After an abuser is removed from the home, parent/caretaker must go back to work. Parent's/Caretaker's view: since she (he) is at work, her (his) teenager should be expected to do all the housework. The teen's view: that she (he) can't be expected to do housework, her (his) homework, and have any kind of social life. Let the teen practice talking to her (his) parent/caretaker about her (his) feelings. Ask the group for negotiation suggestions.

Scenario #2: After the abuse is disclosed, a parent/caretaker has trouble letting her (his) teen out of her (his) sight, and will hardly let her (him) have any privileges. Parent's/Caretaker's view: she (he) is so frightened that something else bad will happen that she (he) needs to have the girl (boy) with her (him) at all times. Teen's view: she (he) needs more freedom. Play out a negotiation where the teen helps parent/caretaker to feel more safe, but asks for more freedom.

Scenario #3: The stepfather (stepmother) who abused the teen has been in treatment and says he (she) is better. He (She) wants to come back for visits to the home. Parent's/Caretaker's view: she (he) and the family's other children want to see him (her), as he (she) always brings gifts and acts very nice. Teen's view: she (he) does not feel safe around her (his) stepfather (stepmother). How can the teen negotiate with parent/caretaker and family so that she (he) feels safe and feels that her (his) siblings are safe also?

Therapists can use these and other scenarios to assist group members who need help with specific situations at home. Therapists will want to consider whether to have parents/caretakers at this session; their attendance can be extremely helpful, providing excellent opportunities for parents/caretakers and children to practice negotiating. Parents/Caretakers often suggest activities for negotiation, offering to role-play with their children/wards the situations that represent their actual conflicts and problem areas.

Steps 4 through 8. As previously discussed.

Purpose:

To provide opportunities for awareness/acknowledgment of feelings, and to teach relaxation as a coping technique.

Materials Needed:

Role basket, Homework Assignment #9, galvanic skin response (GSR) machine(s) (optional), and refreshments.

Format:

1. Role selection.
2. Homework review.
3. Session task: relaxation and thought-stopping techniques.
4. Group cheer.
5. Summarization.
6. Refreshment and clean-up.
7. Homework assignment.
8. Positive feedback good-byes.

Contents of Session Ten

Steps 1 to 2. As previously discussed.

3. *Session Task: Cognitive, Biofeedback, and Relaxation Techniques for Dealing with Feelings and Intrusive Thoughts.* As discussed in Part I and in Chapter 10 of Part III, we provide our group members with brief training in cognitive techniques (visualization, "thought-stopping," etc.), relaxation training, and use of simple biofeedback techniques.

    Although not essential, it is useful to possess and use for this session at least one galvanic skin response machine: a simple, hand-held instrument that measures the degree of relaxation or stress shown by a subject. A number of kits are available from commercial suppliers; they are typically sold with simple relaxation training tapes containing instructions for use. Although we describe relaxation training fully in this session (below), it is typically conducted in several learning segments. Subsequent sessions should allow time for practice.

    (a) *Visualization (Cognitive Training).* Each member is asked to think of a simple scene that she (he) finds very relaxing, and which she (he) can visualize in her (his) "mind's eye," with her (his) eyes closed. She (He) should be alone in this scene, and it should be a place where she (he) feels perfectly safe, relaxed, and pleasant. Some of our members' chosen situations have included lying on a beach, floating in a pool on a large rubber float, or sitting in a swing on a porch. With eyes closed so that she (he) can "see" it, each member in turn describes her (his) scene to the rest of the group.

    (b) *Selecting a "Mantra" or Phrase for Thought-Stopping.* Members are advised that, once they have visualized their relaxing scenes, they can fill their minds with a simple word or phrase in order to "thought-stop," or remove anxiety-provoking images or thoughts. Each member is asked to think of a simple, soothing word, or "mantra" that she (he) can repeat over and over to herself (himself). Suggestions include strong; I'm strong; safe; I'm safe; I'll be happy and successful; I'm a good, strong person. Some teens invariably wish to use the name of their current boyfriend (girlfriend), in which case therapists explain that stimulating words or images are not effective.

After practicing saying her (his) word or phrase aloud to the rest of the group, each member is instructed to close her (his) eyes and hear herself (himself) saying it in her (his) mind.

(c) *Deep Breathing Exercises.* Members' medical charts and information should be reviewed to ascertain whether any unusual breathing or other physical patterns might pose any danger or difficulty for them. Although unlikely, it is possible that breathing or muscle-tensing exercises might be contraindicated for members with some types of migraines, low seizure thresholds, current medications, or other physical difficulties.

Members are shown how to take three deep breaths through the nose, hold them to the count of five, and then release through the mouth in a slow manner to the count of five. Members practice taking these three deep breaths and then sitting quietly, breathing as if they were about to go to sleep, while they visualize their safe places and scenes.

(d) *Muscle Relaxation Exercises* (check medical records first). We teach progressive relaxation in the following manner. Group members sit in comfortable chairs with arms by their sides. The therapist instructs them to begin with the tops of their heads and their foreheads, making them as tight as possible. Progressing downward, they are asked to tighten the muscles around their eyes and mouths, squeezing them and gritting their teeth, then to include necks and chests. Next, shoulders, arms, and hands should be clenched as tightly as possible. Stomachs should be pulled in tightly. Finally, thighs are squeezed together, calves tightened, and feet and toes are squeezed and tightened. Therapist tells group members to hold these tensions to the count of five.

Progressively, starting with the toes, members are told to release the muscle tension, moving upward from feet and legs, through chest, arms, and face and neck.

(e) *Combining the Techniques.* This is where the practical application of all the techniques is integrated. Each member is asked to name a thought or worry that she (he) often experiences. The group then practices replacing the words about that thought with their "mantras," repeating the "mantras" to themselves 10 times. Some members have said that they need to say their "mantras" out loud to stop the thoughts, and should be allowed to do so. They should be reminded to continue practicing saying their "mantras" silently, however, so that the technique will be available to them in a public environment.

Next, members practice the muscle tightening/relaxation progression three times, ending the practice by sitting in a "floppy," relaxed posture. They are instructed to follow the muscle relaxation with three deep breaths, again concluding by sitting in the same "floppy," relaxed posture. Finally, they begin to visualize their safe, relaxed scenes while trying to breathe, "like you were just about to go to sleep."

Biofeedback or GSR kit instructions may include variations of the preceding exercises. One advantage of their use is that they help group members measure and select the techniques which were most effective for them individually.

The importance of practicing these techniques should be thoroughly emphasized and included in the homework for this session. If parents or caretakers attend this group session, it is important to encourage them to practice the techniques with their children at home.

Steps 4 through 8. As previously discussed.

SESSION ELEVEN

Purpose:

To practice relaxation techniques, rehearse didactic material, review, and enhance self-esteem and self-awareness.

Materials Needed:

Role basket, a list of key points about sexual abuse written on chalkboard or easel (optional, see below), *That Was Then, But This Is Now* booklets, clipboards, pencils, Homework Assignment #10, and refreshments.

Format:

1. Role selection.
2. Homework review.
3. Relaxation practice.
4. Session task: role-play: I'm My Own Grandma (Grandpa).
5. Therapists' requests for input concerning future groups like this one.
6. Group cheer.
7. Summarization.
8. Refreshments and clean-up.
9. Homework assignment.
10. Positive feedback good-byes.

Contents of Session Eleven

Steps 1 to 2. As previously discussed.

3. *Relaxation Practice.* The session may begin with a rehearsal of relaxation exercises from the last meeting and a review of Homework Assignment #9, in which members are asked to practice the exercises and to write down their experiences.

4. *Session Task: Rehearsal of Learning with Role-Play, "I'm My Own Grandma (Grandpa)."* Group members are reminded and assured how much wiser and stronger they are than when the group started. The therapist may begin, "People your age who have never had to deal with anything bad happening to them are lucky in a way. But in a way they are not lucky, because they have not had a chance to develop the skills which you have learned about dealing with feelings and difficult and confusing situations. When they are adults, they may have a difficult time dealing with the hard things that all adults go through, like losing somebody through death or divorce, or having to cope with a situation in which they are treated badly.

"But you have learned that 'That was then, but this is now.' You have become strong survivors, and you can teach the things you learned to others. In this session we are going to pretend that we are grown up — so grown up, in fact, that we are grandmothers (grandfathers) with 7-year-old granddaughters (grandsons), and we are going to tell them about sexual abuse." (Instruct group members to write down what they want to teach their grandchildren.)

Beginning with the members who chose the *Group Actor* role cards, members take turns playing grandmother (grandfather) and granddaughter (grandson). Each "grandmother" ("grandfather") decides what she (he) wants to tell her "granddaughter" ("grandson") about sexual abuse. She (He) may or may not want to say that she (he) has been abused herself (himself), but if she (he) does choose to say this, she (he) must add, "but I learned how to deal with my feelings, and how to protect myself and get help, and I was never abused again."

Members usually have fun deciding what they would like their granddaughters' (grandsons') names to be, and usually decide to reveal that they have been abused, but that they grew up stronger because of what they learned about handling their feelings.

A typical role-play begins with a statement such as: "When I was your age (or a little older), I had some bad touches that were called sexual abuse. I was very upset by this, and I was in a group of other girls (boys) where I learned how to handle my feelings and how to protect myself and get help, and I was never abused again. In some ways it made me stronger. But I would like you to learn about these things before something like this ever happens to you, because it is a hard thing to go through, and I don't want you to go through it. Here are some things you should know."

The following points should be included by each "grandmother" ("grandfather"). Therapists may wish to have a brief chart with key words for the group to follow in their talk with their grandchild.

- Bad touches and your rights: Tell what a bad touch is and emphasize that nobody, even a member of your family, is allowed to give you a bad touch because your body is yours and is private.
- Situations that might lead to bad touches: Give some examples of ways for granddaughters (grandsons) to keep themselves safe, both from strangers and even from family members and friends.
- How to get help and tell someone: Emphasize telling people until someone stops the abuse or the situation that is frightening to you.
- Some people are good in some ways and bad in others: Give a brief explanation of how people who abuse children have problems in their minds, even though they may do good things for you at times. But older people know that they should not give bad touches, and they should be made to stop.
- It is never the child's fault when she or he gets a bad touch: Explain that older people know better, and that it is against the law. It is never the child's fault, and a child should not feel bad about telling about the abuse.
- People can get over their bad feelings about being abused: Most members choose to reveal that they had a bad touch, but then add that they learned how to handle their feelings about it, learned how to protect themselves and get help, and were not abused again.
- Any questions? The "granddaughter" ("grandson") is allowed to ask any questions she (he) thinks the child she (he) is portraying in the role-play might want to know. The group and therapists can also make suggestions for answering the questions.

5. *Therapists' Requests for Suggestions.* At the end of the session, members are asked to discuss and write in their booklets any issues or areas they think groups like this might include in the future and which they believe were not adequately covered in their group.

Steps 6 through 10. As previously discussed.

SESSION TWELVE

Purpose:

To provide closure, reinforce self-esteem, provide transition objects or activities, administer posttest, and celebrate graduation.

Materials Needed:

Posttest and pencils, refreshments, small gifts or "transition objects," graduation certificates, tape recorder and "graduation music," Polaroid camera and film, and completed booklets and homework assignments, stapled together, one for each member.

Format:

1. Role selection.
2. Homework review and discussion.
3. Posttesting.
4. Graduation.
5. Presentation of member booklets and transition objects.
6. Cheers and chants.
7. Refreshments.
8. Clean-up.
9. Positive feedback good-byes.

Contents of Session Twelve

Steps 1 to 2. As previously discussed.

3. *Posttesting.* It is helpful to handle this chore outside of therapy sessions, but often this is administratively impossible. The most time-effective method for administering the posttest in session is for therapists to read the questions while members fill in the answer sheets. Therapists should monitor to see that all members are on the correct question lines on the answer sheet.

4. *Graduation.* In our groups, therapists usually play an appropriate tape on a tape player, call out each member's name, invite her (him) to walk to the front of the group, and present her (him) with her (his) graduation certificate by reading it aloud. Having parents or caretakers attend makes this occasion more formal and important.

5. *Presentation of the Booklets and Transition Objects.* Each member's booklet is presented, and each contains a personal note from the therapist on the last page, congratulating her (him) and listing the areas on which she (he) may wish to continue to work. A phone number and address for contacting the therapist or agency in the future should be included.

   It is valuable to present each member with a small, inexpensive "transition object" by which to remember the group, and to which she (he) (or therapist) may attach her (his) specific "mantra." In many of our groups we have been able to secure funds for a simple silver bracelet, earrings, or pin. Members are encouraged to touch their transition objects at least once a week, while they repeat their "mantras" or a chant such as, "I'm a good person, I'm proud of me. I've been through a lot, but look how strong I've got!"

In lieu of financial expenditure, it is possible to give each member an envelope in which therapists have placed a number of small strips of paper similar to those found in fortune cookies, on which are written chants and cheers, self-esteem statements, and statements of encouragement. These can be pulled from the envelope and read when a member needs some reinforcement of group learning. She (He) should read the slip, return it to the envelope, and repeat a cheer to herself (himself).

As with younger groups, it is also enjoyable for each member to receive a Polaroid photo of herself (himself), taken on the day of her (his) graduation. During this last session therapists should encourage an atmosphere of accomplishment, celebration, and mutual support.

Steps 6 through 9. As previously discussed.

Note: As stated following the sessions for younger groups, follow-up contact after the last group is extremely important. We attempt to contact parents or caretakers 2 weeks, 3 months, and 1 year following the last group session.

CHAPTER 13

Guide to Supplemental Material for Teen's Groups Ages 13 to 16

The following is a listing of the materials that can be found in Part IV.

THEMES IN THE ACTIVITY BOOK

Pages	Themes
G1	Cover
G3	My Three Wishes (use with Session Two).
G4	Three Things I Need Band-Aids For (Session Three).
G5	Things I Want to Work On the Most (Session Three).
G6	Rules We Use in This Group (Session Three).
G7	The Things I Would Like to See Added to the *"Wouldn't It Be Nice"* Coloring Book (Session Three).
G8	"Mirror, Mirror On the Wall" (Session Five).
G9	A Letter to the Person Who Sexually Abused Me (Session Seven).
G10	Ten Good Things About Me (Session Eight)
G11	Three Ways Abuse Made Me Feel Bad About Myself (Session Eight)
G12	Rules for Negotiation (Session Nine).
G13	Learning the Rules for Negotiating (Session Nine).
G14	Notes About Relaxation (Session Ten).
G15	What I Will Teach My Granddaughter (Grandson) (Session Eleven).
G16	What I Need to Work On (Session Twelve).
G17	What Should Be Included in Future Groups (Session Eleven).
G18	A Special Note for You From _____ (Session Twelve)

COMMENTS AND THEMES REGARDING HOMEWORK ASSIGNMENTS

Assignments	Pages	Themes
#1	H3	Three wishes (use with Session Two).
#2	H4	Critique of the coloring book *"Wouldn't It Be Nice"* (Session Three).
#3	H5	Myths about sexual abuse (Session Four).

Assignments	Pages	Themes (Cont'd)
#4	H6	A question I have never asked my parent/caretaker but wanted to (Session Five).
#5	H7	Talking with my parent/caretaker about taking care of myself (Session Six).
#6	H8	How my parent/caretaker and I visualize me when I am 21 (Session Seven).
#7	H9	Three things I like about my parent/caretaker and three things she (he) likes about me (Session Eight).
#8	H10-H11	Negotiation practice (Session Nine).
#9	H12	Relaxation practice (Session Ten).
#10	H13	Ways I have gotten stronger (Session Eleven).

ADDITIONAL ITEMS

Pages	Items
I1-I5	*The Life Game* and game cards (in this game you may also use the Learning Cards for the *Moving On and Getting Stronger Game*).
J1	Game Cards.
J3-J8	Learning Cards.
J9-J15	Understanding Each Other Cards.
J16-J22	Knowing Yourself Cards.
J23-J28	Problem-Solving Cards.
K1-K4	Graduation Certificates.

SUPPLEMENTAL MATERIAL

Table of Contents for
Materials for Ages 6 to 12

Table of Contents for
Materials for Ages 13 to 16

My Very Own

"Wouldn't It Be Nice"

Coloring Book

My Name: _____

Wouldn't It Be Nice If . . .

Wouldn't it be nice if you took your vitamins and ate good food and exercised, and you could keep from <u>ever</u> getting sick.

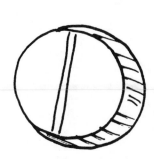

Vitamin

Color and "name" the vitamin
(A, B, C, D, E)

Color the Tomato

But The Way It Really Is . . .

The way it really is, even if you do all these things, sometimes a germ can come along and you will get sick. <u>Everybody</u> gets sick sometimes.

Germ

Draw a Germ

(Make one up . . . a really ugly one.)

What We Can Do About It . . .

We can eat right and exercise and take vitamins and get plenty of sleep and then we <u>don't get sick very often</u>. And when we do get sick, we don't stay sick very long.

Color him feeling better again.

Wouldn't It Be Nice If . . .

Wouldn't it be nice if children would grow up and never have an adult or older person touch them in a wrong, bad way. Or make them do things to the adult's private parts which are a wrong, bad touch. Wouldn't it be nice if all touches were nice, right touches.

Name a nice, right, good touch.   **Name a wrong, bad touch.**

_____   _____

But The Way It Really Is . . .

You are not the only child who has had a wrong, bad touch. There are many, many girls and boys who have had this happen to them. When this happens, it is called sexual abuse.

Color one face for you.

What We Can Do About It . . .

If somebody tries to give you a wrong, bad touch, or tries to make you give them a wrong, bad touch, or wants to talk in a funny way to you about it, or tries to show you pictures of a wrong, bad touch . . . this is sexual abuse and this is what we can do about it.

1. First, we need to learn to tell a bad, wrong touch from a good, nice touch. A bad, wrong touch is when someone touches your private parts, or makes you touch his or her private parts, or wants you to talk about bad touches in a funny way, or wants to show you pictures of bad touches.

2. We can learn how to say no to a bad, wrong touch, and learn how to get away. You need to say real loud: NO, I DON'T WANT TO DO THAT! I'M GOING TO TELL MY PARENT/ CARETAKER! STOP! Then run away and find somebody to tell if you can.

3. We can learn how to tell somebody who will make the adult stop the abuse. At home you could tell your mother or caretaker. At school you could tell you teacher or principal or counselor. Or you might tell your minister or somebody you trust. You should keep on telling people until somebody makes the abuse stop. You can even call the police, any time of day, at 911, and tell them you are being sexually abused and you want it to stop.

4. We can learn that it is the adult or older person's fault. Abuse is not the child's fault. The older person knows better. They know a child is too young to be able to understand or handle sexual touches and feelings. And they know it is against the law to do this.

5. You can learn to talk about your feelings and about what happened to your mother or caretaker or special helping people, like a therapist or counselor, and they can help you keep from worrying and feeling bad about the abuse.

6. You can learn to feel good about yourself and learn how to feel safe again. And you can learn that you are not alone, and that abuse happens to many, many children. You can grow up to be a happy, strong person like many people who have been abused and who got help with their feelings.

7. You can go to a special therapy person or be in a group like this one, where you will work on learning all these things, how to tell a bad, wrong touch, how to help keep yourself from being abused by saying "No" and "Stop" — "I'm going to tell someone." "I don't want to do this." And you can learn how to find someone to tell about it, how to talk about your feelings, and how what happened was not your fault. And how to feel good about yourself and feel safe.

Color yourself feeling smart . . . because you are learning all these things.

Wouldn't It Be Nice If . . .

Wouldn't it be nice if all the adults and children in your family were happy all the time and didn't have any problems.

But The Way It Really Is . . .

The way it really is, people sometimes have really bad problems inside themselves. They are mixed up about the way they feel about things, and about what is right and wrong. Sometimes they look okay outside, but have the really bad problems inside. Sometimes even the people in our own families have problems inside themselves, and these problems can make them do wrong things.

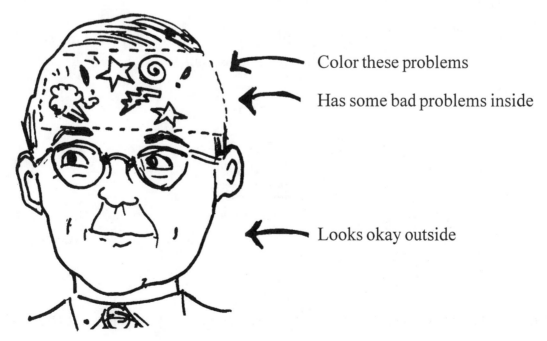

What We Can Do About It . . .

What we can do about it is . . .

1. We can know that even if a person has problems, and that is the reason they abuse children, they cannot keep on doing it because it hurts children and upsets them — and it is against the law.

2. We can learn how to say "No. Stop. Don't do that. I'm going to tell."

3. Grownups are supposed to keep kids safe, and they are supposed to know right from wrong. If they sexually abuse children, a child can say "No. Stop. Don't do that. I'm going to tell."

Name some people you can tell who could make the person stop the abuse.

       At home you could tell: _____

       At school you could tell: _____

       At church you could tell: _____

4. If nobody does anything to make the abuse stop, you can call the police any time of the day or night.

    You can pick up the phone and call 911.

    Practice using the phone (pretend) in the group. Call 911, and say:

    "Hello . . . This is (<u>your name</u>). I live at (<u>your address</u>). My telephone number is (<u>your number</u>).

    Somebody is doing bad things, like sexual abuse to me, and I am scared. Please get somebody to help me. I need help."

Call 911

Wouldn't It Be Nice . . .

Wouldn't it be nice if . . . <u>when</u> you were very, very good and tried to be the best person you could be, then nothing bad would happen to you.

**Draw a halo
and color it.**

But The Way It Really Is . . .

The way it really is . . . no matter how good you are, or how good you try to be, bad things happen to everybody some of the time. Like you can fall and get hurt, and need a Band-Aid. Or an adult or other person can give you a bad touch or do bad things to you that are not your fault. Sometimes bad things like sexual abuse happen to really good people.

Ouch! Color the Band-Aid.

What You Can Do About It . . .

1. You can learn not to blame yourself when bad things get done to you that are not your fault. Like when an adult or other person gives you a bad touch or does bad things to you. It is NOT YOUR FAULT. The adult should know better.

2. Clap hands and say, "I'm a good person! Abuse is not my fault!"

3. You can learn that your private parts (parts usually covered by bathing suits, but your whole body, your mouth, your hands, every part is private to you) belong just to you. Other people cannot even look at your private parts because they belong just to you. The only time someone looks at your private parts is when a real doctor looks to see if your body is well, and your mother or caretaker or a nurse is with you.

4. You are learning that:

You have a right to keep your body private.

5. Say out loud: "My body is private. My body belongs to me. I have a right to keep my body private. Nobody has a right to use it and see it but me."

6. Remember that sometimes bad things happen to good people. A person who has been abused is a good person that has had something bad happen to them which is not their fault. Name some other kinds of bad things that can happen to good people.

    Hints: They could be in a car and have an _____.

                   They could eat some bad food and get _____.

                   They could walk around in a city, and meet up with a mean dog, and the dog could _____ them.

_____

_____

None of these things are the person's fault. Sexual abuse is <u>NOT YOUR FAULT</u>.

Wouldn't It Be Nice . . .

Wouldn't it be nice if every secret someone asked you to keep was a good secret, like what they were getting somebody else for Christmas, or their birthday. That would be a secret that is okay to keep.

But The Way It Really Is . . .

Sometimes people who sexually abuse someone will try to scare you, and tell you they will hurt you or somebody in your family if you tell the secret about sexual abuse. Or sometimes they promise to give you something really nice, or take you somewhere really nice if you keep the abuse secret.

What We Can Do About It . . .

1. We can learn the difference between good secrets and bad secrets.   Are these secrets bad or good (check one)?

    a. Your friend tells you what she or he got another friend for her or his birthday and tells you not to tell.   ☐ GOOD   ☐ BAD

    b. A person in your family, who could be an uncle, grandfather, or even your own father gives you a bad, wrong touch and tells you not to tell anyone and to keep it a secret.   ☐ GOOD   ☐ BAD

    c. A babysitter looks at your private parts, and makes you look at theirs and takes pictures of your private parts. They tell you to keep this as a special secret. ☐ GOOD   ☐ BAD

2. Tell your mother or caretaker or some of the people we have talked about that someone tried to make you keep a secret that you didn't feel right about. Never let ANYONE make you promise not to tell a secret that makes you feel afraid or mixed up or scared.

> **Say, "I'm not allowed to keep ANY secrets from my parents." or "I have promised to tell my parents anything that somebody tells me, and anything that has to do with somebody touching private parts or talking about them."**

Wouldn't It Be Nice . . .

Wouldn't it be nice if you could feel safe all the time, and you knew everybody around you was a safe person.

Color yourself wishing you could feel safe always.

But The Way It Really Is . . .

It is hard to tell who is a safe person.   Sometimes children get abused by someone in their family, or somebody they trust, like a teacher or babysitter.

SAFE?   **NOT SAFE?**

Color the question mark and the people.

What We Can Do About It . . .

The way it really is, we have to try to learn who is a safe person and who is not a safe person.

With People You Know . . .

If anybody has ever tried to abuse you by trying to touch your private parts or make you touch them in a strange way, tell your mother or caretaker that you feel funny being with that person, that you don't want to be alone with that person, and tell your mother or caretaker what that person tried to do.

Try to make sure that you are not left alone with that person. Don't let anybody plan things that will leave you alone in the house with that person. Insist on going with your mother or caretaker, and make sure she (he) really understands that you don't feel safe being with this person alone.

If a person — a babysitter, scout leader, or a member of your family — starts to sexually abuse you when you are alone, yell "NO!" Run out of the room and go outside, even to a neighbor's house, and ask for help. Yell and say, "I don't want you to do this. I'm going to tell. STOP!" Don't stay with the person. Run away and get help.

Try to think of a secret code or word you could use with your mother or caretaker. If she (he) ever needed to send someone for you, she (he) would tell that person the secret word. Your homework will be to ask your mother or caretaker to help you make up the code.

With Strangers . . .

You should never accept candy, money, or gifts from strangers who might use that to get to know you. A stranger is somebody you don't know. Never get into a car with a stranger, even if they seem nice.

Do not go off with strangers to look for a dog they say they have lost, or if they ask you to help them find something. Some people lie about this so that they can be alone with you to hurt you. Do not go off with strangers even if they say your mother or caretaker sent them after you, or your mother or caretaker has been hurt and they are taking you to her (him). DO NOT BELIEVE THEM. You and your mother or caretaker can make up a secret code or word that no one else knows. Someone would have to give you the code word before you could leave with them. And even then, it would be best to call your family first.

A14

Wouldn't It Be Nice . . .

Wouldn't it be nice if people could read your mind SOMETIMES. And people who loved you, like your mother or caretaker, could read in your mind that you were worried about sexual abuse without your having to come out and tell her (him), and that she (he) could help you without your saying anything.

Some people think that mothers or caretakers and other people can "just tell" when somebody is being sexually abused, or has had a bad touch. They think other people know about it and wonder why they don't do anything to stop the abuse

Worries

But The Way It Really Is . . .

The way it really is, even people who love you can't read your mind and know that something bad is happening to you. YOU HAVE TO TELL THEM.

What We Can Do About It . . .

1. You have to learn to tell someone and get help for yourself.

2. You have to tell your mother or caretaker or teacher or someone about what has happened and that you are afraid it will happen again.

3. You have to understand that people can't read your mind, or tell what has happened unless you tell them.

> **How many people did you have to tell before somebody did something about the abuse? Fill in how many: _____.**

You just have to keep on telling people if the first one you tell doesn't do anything about it.   Finally somebody will stop the abuse.

Some people get afraid to dress in shorts or take showers in gym class because they think other girls and boys can tell what has happened to them by looking at them. But other people cannot tell by looking at you that you have been sexually abused. Sometimes a special doctor can tell by giving a child a special examination, but sometimes even they can't tell by the examination.

Some girls and boys worry that other people who do not understand that sexual abuse is the adult's fault will think that the child is a bad person for letting the abuse happen. They are afraid other people won't understand how hard it is to tell about the abuse, and will think it is your fault.

> ➢ **Everybody who has thought that people could tell they had been abused hold up your hand.**

> ➢ **Everybody who thought that the abuse happened because they were bad, and it was the child's fault, hold up your hand.**

> ➢ **Everybody who thought there was nothing they could do about the abuse when it first happened, hold up your hand.**

Now everyone clap hands and say together:

"THAT WAS THEN, BUT THIS IS NOW.
I WON'T BE ABUSED, AND I KNOW <u>HOW</u>."

A16

Wouldn't It Be Nice . . .

Wouldn't it be nice if nobody ever tried to hurt you or scare you.

This is a person being afraid somebody might hurt them.

But The Way It Really Is . . .

SOMETIMES PEOPLE WHO ABUSE CHILDREN SAY THAT THEY WILL HURT YOU IF YOU TELL SOMEONE. The person might even say that they would hurt your family or your dog if you tell somebody they are abusing you.

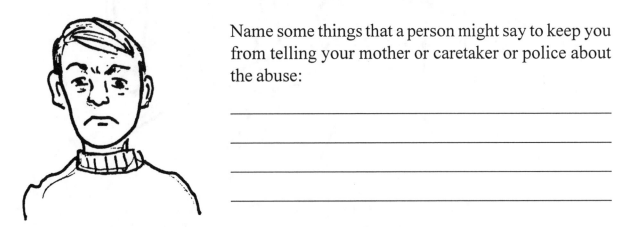

Name some things that a person might say to keep you from telling your mother or caretaker or police about the abuse:

_____

_____

_____

_____

The truth is that they probably won't do anything, because the people who stop the abuse will stop him or her from hurting you or anyone else. You have to tell about the abuse to stop it.

What We Can Do About It . . .

1. You have to tell someone about the abuse, so the person you tell can help get the abuse stopped.

2. Most abusers don't get a chance to hurt a person after the abuse is known to the police and department of social services, because they take the abuser away or take the child to a safe place.

3. Almost all abusers just make things up to scare you and keep you too frightened to tell. They want to keep on doing the abuse, but they would probably be too afraid themselves to hurt someone. That would be too hard to hide and they know they would probably get caught if they really killed or hurt somebody where it would be seen. If <u>you don't tell</u>, sexual abuse is usually easy to hide, and the abusers may not get caught.

4. If <u>you don't tell</u>, not only will you probably keep on being abused, but most abusers go on to abuse other children, sometimes even your own brothers and sisters.

Wouldn't It Be Nice . . .

Wouldn't it be nice if all bad feelings and bad touches were not mixed up with some good feelings and touches, and you could tell right away what was a bad touch. Wouldn't it be nice if people who gave you bad touches didn't also sometimes act very nice to you and keep you mixed up and confused.

But The Way It Really Is . . .

The way it really is, sometimes bad and good feelings about people get all mixed up, and bad and good touches sometimes get mixed up. Sometimes people who abuse children try to touch a child's private parts in a way that will not cause pain, and they also give good touches like hugs or pats on the back.

And sometimes they are very nice to you and give you things and take you to fun places. This makes children feel mixed up about the abuser.

What We Can Do About It . . .

What we can learn and do about it is:

1. We can learn that many children feel two ways about the abuser. Sometimes they really like some things about the abuser, who is good to them in some ways and does some good things for them. But they feel bad and mixed up about the bad touches. No matter how nice someone is to you, he or she does not have the right to give you bad touches, or ask you to give him or her bad touches. And he or she knows that your body and mind are too young to understand sexual touches.

2. A child does not have to feel bad or guilty because she or he has trouble telling the difference between good and bad touches at first. Sometimes the abuser deliberately gives both kinds of touches and is very nice to a child, and tries to confuse the child so she or he will not tell about the bad touch.

3. You have to understand that <u>all your body is your own. Other people do not have the right to touch it or use it.</u>

4. If someone touches or strokes your private parts in a sexual way, it may not hurt in a way that causes physical pain to your body, but it makes you feel mixed up and confused and worried because a child's mind and body are too young and are not ready for these kinds of touches and feelings. Sexual abuse is not right because it makes a child feel confused, mixed up, and that her or his body has not been respected.

Wouldn't It Be Nice . . .

Wouldn't it be nice if, after you told about the bad touches that happened to you, that right away everything would be happy and nice and you wouldn't have any more worries.

But The Way It Really Is . . .

At least one big worry is better. You know that you have told someone about the bad touches and that was the right thing to do.

But most children still have some worries and some bad feelings that they have to handle.

What We Can Do About It . . .

1. List some of the worries and sad and bad feelings you had, even after you told someone about the sexual abuse, and after it got stopped. (Some children say that they are sad it ever happened, mad that they ever trusted the abuser, and afraid that they might get blamed for the abuse happening.)

2. We can tell these sad, mad, and worried feelings to a therapist who will help you with them, or be in a group like this one. You can tell your mother or caretaker or someone else you trust about your feelings. Keeping them inside sometimes makes them grow and get bigger.

3. You can learn that lots of girls and boys have these same kinds of worried, sad, and mad feelings after they have had a bad touch.

4. You can practice talking to yourself about what has happened in your room or when you are by yourself. You can say to yourself:

   > **I did not do anything wrong. It was the adult's fault because they knew they should not do it, and it is against the law for them to abuse a child.**

   > **I am not a bad person because this happened to me. Sexual abuse has happened to thousands of children, and it is not their fault.**

   > **I did not know things I could do to protect myself or get help when this happened before.**

   > **That was THEN. THIS IS NOW, and I have learned ways to protect myself and get help, and not be abused.**

Say the cheer you learned in group:

"THAT WAS THEN, BUT THIS IS NOW
I WON'T BE ABUSED, AND I KNOW <u>HOW!</u>"

Wouldn't It Be Nice . . .

Wouldn't it be nice if, after someone told about being abused, the person who did it would never do it again. They would just promise or sign a contract that they would never abuse another child, and then a magic wand would make everything all right, and everyone would be happy.

But The Way It Really Is . . .

The way it really is, most sexual abusers, even if they say they will stop, will keep on abusing children unless they get some special help, or are put in jail away from children. So sometimes a child is taken away from a home where there is a sexual abuser, to protect the child, and sometimes the sexual abuser is put in jail, to keep him or her from abusing again.

What We Can Do About It . . .

1. If you don't tell about the abuse, the abuser will probably keep on doing the abusing, and that is not good for you, or for other children they may abuse.

2. The person who is abusing you may also abuse other children, and you might have prevented this by telling about your abuse.

3. People who sexually abuse children really know it is a wrong and bad thing to do. Some of them want to stop doing the abuse, but they can't. They need help to stop doing it, and the only way they can get help is when you tell someone who will stop the abuse and make them get the help they need.

4. Sometimes people don't tell about the abuse, because in some other ways the abuser is nice to them, and they are afaid that the abuser will have to go to jail. But jail may be the only place where someone can get treatment for being a sexual abuser. And sometimes sexual abusers feel very bad about what they are doing, because in their hearts they know what they are doing is wrong, and hurts children.

5. You have a right to tell. Abuse worries and upsets you, and makes you feel bad about yourself, and gives you angry and mixed-up feelings.

Wouldn't It Be Nice . . .

Wouldn't it be nice if we knew just how to cure people who abused children and what exactly made them do the sexual abuse. Wouldn't it be nice if we could just give them a pill or a shot and they would be cured and would never do it again.

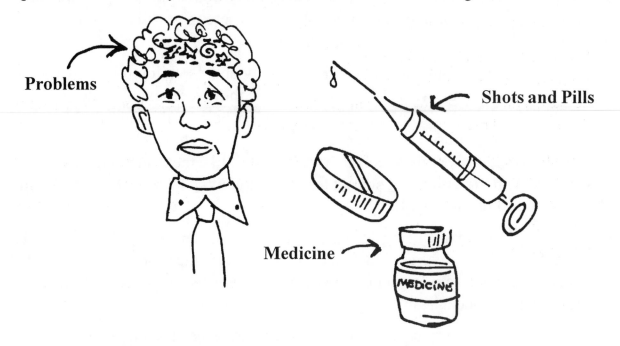

But The Way It Really Is . . .

But the way it really is, it is <u>very hard</u> to cure sexual abusers. It is <u>very hard</u> for sexual abusers to change.

What We Can Do About It . . .

We do not know exactly what causes people to sexually abuse children. And it is hard to cure them.

Sometimes people are in therapy to help them change. Sometimes they are willing to go to therapy, and sometimes they are sent to jail where they will have to get treatment, and children will be protected from them.

1. We can understand that a person who sexually abuses children has a very bad problem inside themselves. Maybe it is because they were sexually abused themselves when they were children, and they never got help for this, and always stayed mixed-up and confused about sexual feelings. Maybe they do not feel safe with other adults, or maybe they feel other adults won't like them and that only a child can like them. These are <u>not normal feelings for adults.</u> This means that the adult has serious problems.

2. A serious problem like being a sexual abuser does not go away quickly or easily, even if the adult wants very much to change. Because these problems are hard to change, we cannot always believe it when the abuser says things like, "I'm sorry, and I will never do it again."

3. You must still be very careful around someone who has tried to abuse you, and follow all the rules we learned (not being alone with them, saying, "No, I don't want to do that," etc.).

4. After sexual abuse is known, people try to get help for the sexual abuser, and some of them do finally get better. But it takes a long time, and we need for children to keep safe while the abuser is getting help. Sometimes the abuser has to go to jail to get help. <u>It is not the child's fault if the abuser has to go to jail.</u> The abusers know that sexual abuse of a child is not right, and that it is against the law. They should have gotten help for themselves and not have done the sexual abuse. It is the abusers' own fault that they were sent to jail, because they broke the law, and children need to be protected from abuse.

A26

Wouldn't It Be Nice . . .

Wouldn't it be nice if you never had to think about the abuse again after it got stopped and the abuser was taken away. Wouldn't it be nice if you never had to worry or feel sad again.

Only Happy Memories

But The Way It Really Is . . .

For a while, even after the abuse stops, children may have bad dreams about the abuse, or have angry feelings that it ever happened.

What We Can Do About It . . .

1. Children can talk to their parents/caretakers and a therapist or special counselor, or be in a group like this one to let their feelings out and to learn ways to handle their feelings.

2. Children can learn how to "talk to themselves" and say all the things we have learned in our group, like, "I'm a good person. The abuse was not my fault. That was then but this is now. I won't be abused and I KNOW HOW!"

3. They can draw pictures about their feelings, just the way we did in the group, or write down their feelings to get them out.

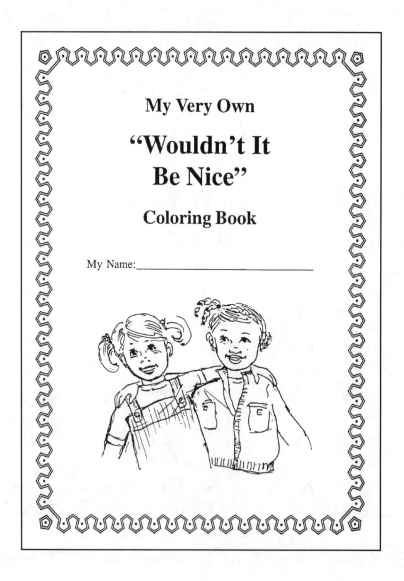

My Very Own

"Wouldn't It Be Nice"

Coloring Book

My Name:_____

Wouldn't It Be Nice . . .

Wouldn't it be nice if children who have been abused could learn to feel good about themselves, that the abuse was not their fault, that they are not alone (thousands and thousands of other children have been abused), and that they could grow up to be happy adults who can teach their own children how to keep from being abused.

But The Way It Really Is . . .

The way it really is, <u>all this is true</u>. Children can learn with the help of their parents, caretakers, and therapists that they are good people, the abuse was not their fault, and they can learn to handle their sad and mad feelings and grow up to be happy adults. It usually takes some time before these feelings all get better, but many people have gone through this and become happy and successful. We talked about some people in the group who told about their abuse as a child, like TV stars, movie stars, and famous beauty queens.

YOU ARE GOING TO LEARN TO HANDLE YOUR FEELINGS TOO, AND GROW UP TO BE A STRONGER, HAPPIER PERSON. REMEMBER YOUR CHEER.

I'VE BEEN THROUGH A LOT, BUT LOOK HOW STRONG I'VE GOT!

Feeling Faces

INSTRUCTIONS

These are eight separate drawings printed two per page. Photocopy each page on one side of card stock and then cut into two separate cards with one face per card.

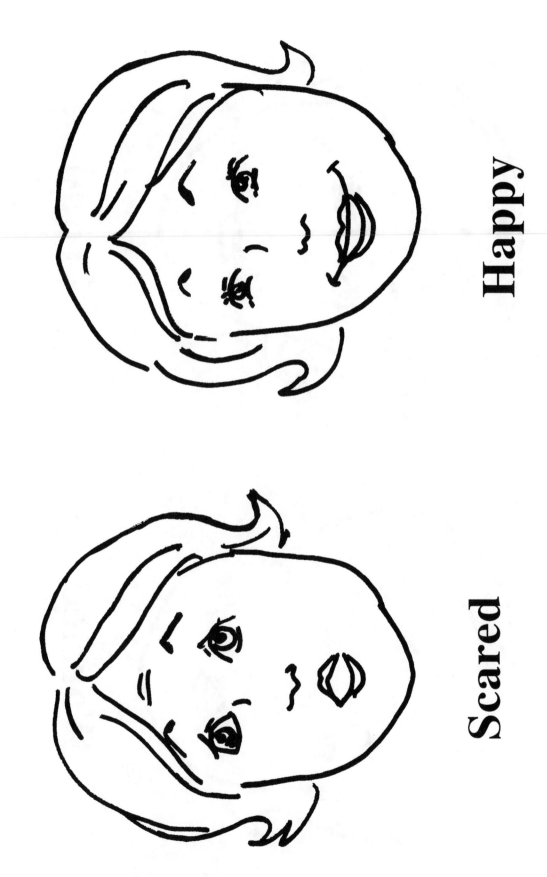

Happy

Scared

B3

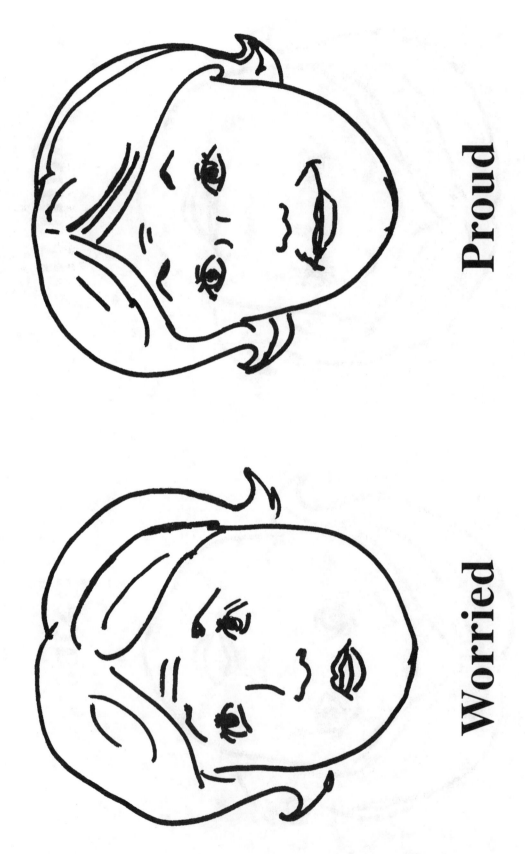

Proud

Worried

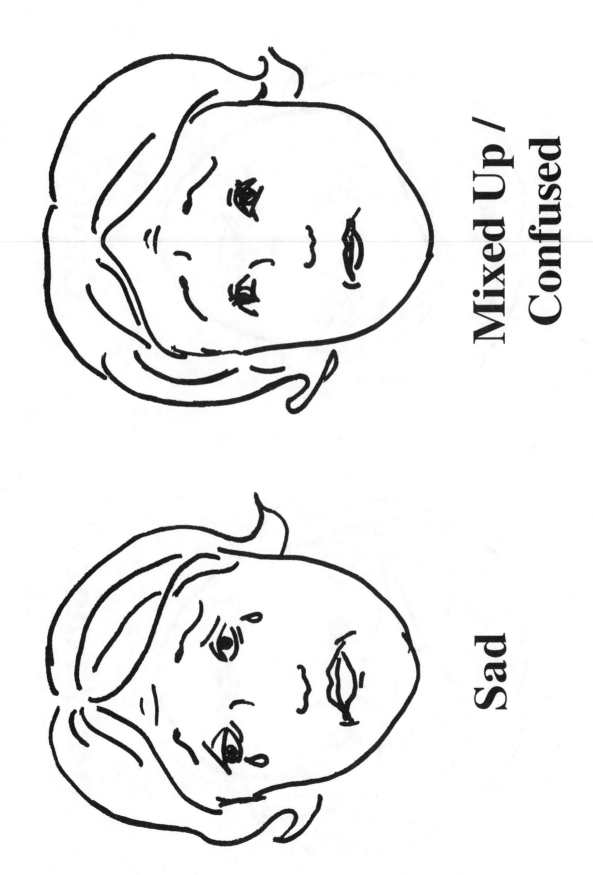

**Mixed Up /
Confused**

Sad

Guilty

Mad / Angry

"Draw-A-Picture" Sheets

INSTRUCTIONS

These are six separate drawings. Photocopy full size. These sheets may be printed double-sided on the paper. In other words, there can be one drawing on one side of the page and another drawing on the back side.

Draw a picture of something that happened to you that made you have this feeling.

Sad Feeling

Draw a picture of something that happened to you that made you have this feeling.

Scared Feeling

Draw a picture of something that happened to you that made you have this feeling.

Safe Feeling

Draw a picture of something that happened to you that made you have this feeling.

Guilty Feeling

Draw a picture of something that happened to you that made you have this feeling.

Mad/Angry Feeling

Draw a picture of something that happened to you that made you have this feeling.

Happy Feeling

Homework Assignments
For Ages 6 to 12

HOMEWORK ASSIGNMENT #1
(Assign During Session Two)

Directions: Go over this homework with your mother or caretaker. You will be teaching her (him) what you learned in your group and practicing what you learned. She (He) will help you read the homework.

Dear Mother (or Caretaker):

In my special group I have learned these things. (See if your mother or caretaker can fill in the blanks. You can help.)

1. I learned what sexual abuse is. Sexual abuse is when an adult or older person gives a child a _____ touch, on their _____ parts, or has the child touch their _____ parts in a way that makes the child feel bad or scared.

2. I learned the difference between a nice, good touch, and a bad, wrong touch. A nice, good touch is when your _____ gives you a hug or a friend gives you a pat on the shoulder. A touch that is a bad or wrong touch is when anybody touches your private parts in a way that makes you feel _____. Only when you were a baby and had to be bathed or when your mother or caretaker takes you to the doctor should *anybody* be touching your _____ parts. Your body is private, and you are the only one who owns it. Other people do not have the _____ to touch your body.

3. I learned that abuse happens to _____ of girls and boys, and I am not the only one. Some people say that sexual abuse happens to one girl in every five. That means that there are hundreds and thousands of children who have been abused.

4. I learned that sexual abuse is not the fault of the _____. It is the _____ of the adult or older person, because he (she) knows you are not supposed to do this to children. He (She) knows he (she) will get in trouble with the police, because it is against the law.

5. I learned who you can tell if you get abused. You can tell your _____ at home, or your _____ at school, or your _____ at church or temple. Or you can tell the police by calling _____.

HOMEWORK ASSIGNMENT #2
(Assign During Session Three)

Directions: Go over this homework with your mother or caretaker. Have her (him) read it out loud and see if you two can fill in the blanks. Help your mother or caretaker with what you have learned in the group.

1. Today in the group we learned that sometimes bad things can happen to you, even if you are a good person and try very hard to be really _____.

2. One thing that happens to good girls and boys sometimes is that adults and older people sexually _____ them. This is not the child's fault, because the adults and older people know better. They know that a child is too young to understand and deal with these kinds of feelings and touches.

3. We do not know exactly what makes adults sexually abuse children, but we know that people who sexually abuse children have bad _____ inside themselves, even if they look okay on the outside, and seem nice in some other ways.

4. But even if the adults have problems, they do not have the right to abuse children, and they have to stop this. We learned some ways to get people to stop. First the child can say "_____" and "_____," and "I will tell my _____. I don't want to do this."

5. If they won't stop, children can try to _____ from them. Then they can tell their _____ at home, or their _____ at school. They should keep on telling people until someone can get the abuse stopped. If no one will help, they can go to the phone and call the police at _____. When you call the police at 911 they will answer the phone no matter what time it is. This is what you should say to the police:

    _____

    _____

Did you help your mother or caretaker with the answers? You were smart to know them all. You and your mother or caretaker can give yourselves a good hug after you go through all the homework and get it right.

HOMEWORK ASSIGNMENT #3
(Assign During Session Four)

Directions to Mother or Caretaker: You and your child should read this together and fill in the blanks. This homework covers some of the things we are learning about in our group.

1. We have learned that there are two kinds of secrets. There are _____ secrets and _____ secrets. A kind of good secret would be _____. A bad secret would be _____.

PLEASE READ THIS OUT LOUD TO YOUR CHILD:
"I always want you to tell me if somebody tries to touch your private parts, or have you touch his or hers, or if somebody scares you by talking about these things. I always want you to tell me, and I will not be mad at you, because these things are not your fault."
---

2. It would be a good thing if a child would make a _____ to her mother/caretaker not to keep any bad secrets.

3. We learned some ways to keep safe from strangers:

    *   You should never take _____ or _____ from strangers.
    *   You should never get in a _____ or go off with strangers.
    *   You should never go with strangers, even if they said your mother or caretaker sent them and wants you to go.

Make up a code word or phrase for your child which would be a good secret between the two of you. The stranger would have to know the secret code word before your child would believe him (her) that you wanted your child to go with him (her).
---

4. Even if the stranger knew the secret word, it would be best to call your mother or caretaker before you went anywhere that was not planned with someone.

5. Never go off with a stranger to look for his (her) _____ or something he (she) says he (she) has lost and needs your help to find.

6. Don't play alone in an empty _____, or go off in an unusual place alone.

7. We also learned how to keep safe with people in our family or people we know. Even if you know someone or he (she) is in your family, he (she) should never try to sexually abuse you. You should tell your _____ what he (she) did and ask your mother or caretaker to never leave you _____ with him (her), no matter who he (she) is.

8. If someone tries to abuse you when you are alone with him (her) in your house, you should say "_____" and "_____" and try to run and tell somebody, or ask for help.

9. You should ask that nothing be planned which would leave you alone with that person. You should tell your mother or caretaker, "I don't feel _____ being alone with that person."

PRACTICE THE GOOD SECRET CODE WORD THAT THE TWO OF YOU MADE UP!

HOMEWORK ASSIGNMENT #4
(Assign During Session Five)

Directions: This is a review of the things we have been learning and talking about in the group.

1. People who abuse children often feel bad about doing it, but they have trouble _____ them-selves from doing it. That is one reason that children should tell about being sexually abused. The person who is sexually abusing may have to get _____ to quit abusing children.

2. Sometimes it is very scary for the child to tell about the sexual abuse, because she (he) is scared that maybe the person will have to go to _____ to get any help and stop abusing children. And sometimes if the abuser is willing to get help, he (she) can get the _____ he (she) needs from therapy programs and from social services.

3. Sometimes children are afraid to tell about sexual abuse because they are afraid they will be _____ from their parents and their homes. Sometimes that can happen, at least for a while. But when things change, and the abuse stops, they will get to go back to their homes.

4. The *main* reason a child needs to know that she (he) should tell about the abuse is the abuse can make children feel _____ about themselves, and give them worries for a _____ time. Chil-dren are too young to understand and handle sexual feelings and touches. The worries and _____ feelings they may have can be helped by going to _____ or social services or someplace which has a special group for helping abused children. But the abuse has to stop also. And this may mean taking the abuser away from the _____ .

5. Sometimes children get mixed up about abuse and bad touches, since the abuser may also be very nice to them at other times. Sometimes an abuser gives both _____ touches and _____ touches. This is one of the reasons sexual abuse is _____ for children. It mixes them up and confuses them, and can make them feel _____ about themselves.

6. One of the other reasons a child needs to tell about sexual abuse is that all children need to learn to take care of themselves, or they may be taken advantage of in other ways as they get older. Children have to learn that they have rights, and that their bodies are theirs alone. They have to learn that they can say "_____" and "_____" when someone tries to abuse them, and that they can get help and stand up for themselves. They can learn that they don't have to be a victim, or do things other people want them to that make them feel _____ .

HOMEWORK ASSIGNMENT #5
(Assign During Session Six)

Directions: We have learned some reasons it is hard to tell anybody about sexual abuse. Read some of these reasons out loud together and fill in the blanks.

1. Sometimes a child is too _____ to tell because she (he) thinks no one would believe her (him), because the abuser is good to her (him) and other people in the family in some ways.

2. Sometimes a child is _____ to tell because the abuser has said that if she (he) tells, the abuser will hurt her (him) or someone in the family.

3. Sometimes a child is _____ to tell because she (he) is afraid this will cause a whole lot of trouble for the whole family and that everybody will be _____ at her (him).

4. Sometimes a child is _____ to tell because at first she (he) didn't know what to do. Then if the abuse kept on happening she (he) is _____ that people will think she (he) wanted it to happen. Or that she (he) will be _____ that she (he) didn't tell the first time it happened.

5. Sometimes a child doesn't tell about the abuse, because the abuser tells her (him) that it is okay, that all children do this, and that it is okay to keep secrets just between them, because they are special to each other. These are _____, but a child does not always know they are lies.

SOMETIMES A MOTHER OR CARETAKER HAS TROUBLE BELIEVING THE CHILD RIGHT AWAY BECAUSE . . .

6. It feels so _____ to the mother or caretaker to think that a family member (maybe her husband [his wife] or boyfriend [girlfriend]) could do such a _____ thing to a child.

7. A mother or caretaker feels so _____ that such a thing could happen to her (his) child without her (him) knowing it.

8. She (He) is _____ that the whole family may have to break up because of the abuse, and she (he) knows she (he) might have to take care of the whole family by herself (himself), which is a very _____ job.

9. She (He) has a _____ time understanding why her (his) child didn't tell her (him) the first time it happened because she (he) did not understand all the reasons it is hard for a child to tell about sexual abuse.

D8

EVEN WITH ALL THESE WORRIES, EVERY MOTHER (OR CARETAKER) WANTS HER (HIS) CHILD TO BE _____ FROM SEXUAL ABUSE. SO IT IS VERY, VERY IMPORTANT FOR A CHILD TO TELL HER (HIS) PARENTS ABOUT SEXUAL ABUSE, AND TO TELL OTHER PEOPLE IF PARENTS CANNOT UNDERSTAND.

Parents and Caretakers: **Please tell your children that you are glad now that you know about the abuse, and that they should always tell you if someone tries to abuse them.**

HOMEWORK ASSIGNMENT #6
(Assign During Session Seven)

Directions: These are some of the things we have been talking about in group. Please read aloud and fill in the blanks together.

1. There are many different kinds of people who abuse children. They may look just like anybody else. They do not usually look _____, and you cannot tell just by _____ at them that they would abuse children.

2. Sometimes the sexual abuser may be somebody in your own _____. He (She) could even be somebody living in your own _____. So someone you trust and think is a _____ person, like a babysitter, teacher, scout master, or even a minister, could be a sexual abuser.

3. We do not always understand why people become sexual abusers of children. Sometimes they were sexually _____ themselves when they were children, and somebody they trusted told them this was all right to do.

4. Sometimes sexual abusers do not feel good about themselves and do not think that grown people would like them sexually. They feel safer and stronger if they do sexual things with a young _____.

5. Sometimes sexual abusers are really mixed up in their heads and believe that they are not hurting a child. But normal people know this is wrong, because children are too _____ to understand and deal with sexual acts and feelings.

6. Sometimes people are just mean and don't care if they hurt children, as long as they are doing something they want to do, even if it is against the _____.

7. Sexual abuse has to be stopped because usually if they are not caught, sexual abusers keep right on abusing young _____, even if they promise not to do it again.

8. There are some ways that sexual abusers can be helped, if they really want help. They can go to a _____ program, or be in therapy. Sometimes if they don't want to get help they have to go to _____, where they will be made to go to a treatment program. Children always have a right to be protected from sexual _____.

HOMEWORK ASSIGNMENT #7
(Assign During Session Eight)

Directions: This homework is about feelings abused children sometimes have and what they can do about them, and how parents can help. Please read aloud and fill in the blanks together.

1. Sometimes children who have been sexually abused have _____ and nervous feelings about the abuse. Sometimes they have _____ dreams, and sometimes they have trouble in school, because they spend a lot of time _____ and worrying about the abuse and have trouble paying _____ in class.

2. Sometimes children cry a lot because they feel _____ about being abused and about all the trouble a family has to go through when they have to deal with abuse. Sometimes they may even feel _____, even though the abuse was not their fault.

3. Sometimes children may be grumpy because they feel _____ that the abuse ever happened to them in the first place, and they wish that someone had known about it and made it _____. Sometimes they feel different from other children, if they don't know that abuse happens to lots and lots of _____.

HERE ARE SOME THINGS WE HAVE LEARNED AND TALKED ABOUT THAT HAVE HELPED CHILDREN DEAL WITH SEXUAL ABUSE:

1. They learn that they can talk to their _____ about the abuse and their feelings about it, and that she (he) will try to understand. At school they could talk to a special _____, or they could go to a mental health center or social services department and talk to a special _____, or be in a special _____ with other children who have been abused.

2. They learn to talk to themselves about the abuse. They can say, "The abuse was not my _____. It is always the fault of the _____ because adults know better and know it is not good for children."

3. They learn that they can become a strong person and that they do not have to put up with _____. They learn that there are many people they can go to who will help stop the abuse. They learn that they should keep telling people until somebody gets the _____ stopped.

4. They learn that they are not alone, and that some people think that as many as one out of five girls have been _____. They learn that many famous and rich people were sexually abused when they

were little and still were able to live a _____ life and be successful. Some of the _____ who have talked about being abused on TV and in the newspapers were TV stars, movie stars, and famous beauty queens.

5. They learn that children who have been abused can grow up to be strong, _____ people who do not ever have to be _____ again.

TEACH YOUR MOTHER OR CARETAKER ONE OF THE CHEERS FROM YOUR GROUP:

I'm a good person,
I'm proud of me!
I've been through a lot,
But look how strong I've got!

WANDA'S STORY
(Use With Session Six)

Once upon a time there was a little girl named Wanda. She lived in _____ with her parents. Her parents got a divorce when she was 6, and this made Wanda and her mother very _____. Then 6 months later, her mother met a man named Ralph. He was good to them both and took them out to dinner and the movies and bought them presents. Wanda and her mother felt _____ to have such a nice friend. Then when Wanda was 7, her mother and Ralph decided to get married so that Ralph became her stepfather. The wedding was in a small chapel and Wanda and her mother planned to both wear pretty pink dresses. Wanda was _____ that she was going to be the flower girl and carry a basket of pink roses. When she tried on her pink dress before the wedding, Ralph talked about how beautiful she looked, and he even wanted to help her put on her pink dress. Wanda felt a little _____, because her mother was the only person who had helped her put on her clothes. But her mother said, "I'm _____ that Ralph likes you so much and thinks you are so pretty, and is so good to us both."

They moved to a nice house with blue shutters and a big yard where Ralph put up a swing for her on a big oak tree. For a while everyone was very _____. Then some confusing things started happening. Once when her mother had to work late, Ralph came into the bathroom and wanted to help Wanda with her bath. Nobody had ever done that but her mother and Wanda felt very _____, especially when Ralph even washed her private parts. But he said that it was all right, because she had to be careful to be very clean.

This kept happening more and more, and finally Ralph asked her mother to let him bathe her and help wash her hair so he could feel more like he was her real father. Wanda wanted to tell her mother that she didn't like this and that she was getting some bad touches. But she was _____ her mother would be upset and that Ralph would get mad at her and leave them like her Daddy had done, and then they wouldn't have their nice house and the swing and lots of other things that Ralph gave them.

Then Ralph kept on touching her private parts, and even asked her to touch his private parts in a way that made her _____. She said, "I don't want to do that. I don't understand what you are trying to do, and this makes me feel funny." But Ralph said, "Oh, this is okay, and if you will do these things for me, I will get you a little poodle dog, just the kind of dog you are always saying you want."

Wanda didn't know what to do. It didn't seem right to her, and she had _____ feelings. She thought if she had told her mother everything that was happening when it first started, maybe the bad touches would not have gone this far and her mother would have made Ralph stop. At night she would cry and feel _____ and _____ and _____. Then one day she was so _____ and _____ that she finally went to her mother and said, "I don't know what to do. In some ways Ralph is so nice to me, but he is giving me bad touches and having me touch all his private parts in a way that just doesn't feel right." At first Wanda's mother was so _____ and _____ that she said, "I can hardly believe this. Are you sure you know what you're talking about? Why didn't you tell me in the first place when he first started touching your private parts?" This made Wanda feel very _____ and _____. But when her mother asked more questions and Wanda told everything about how Ralph had her touch his private parts, and how he touched all her private parts, her mother finally believed her, and said, "You did the right thing. I am _____ you came and told me, because you had to be brave to do that. And I am really _____ at Ralph because he did these things to you. People are not supposed to do these things to children. This is sexual abuse when an adult does these things to a child."

Wanda's mother went to her stepfather and told him that he must have really big problems in his mind to do such a thing and that she was very _____ at him. She said that Wanda and she would have to leave if he did not get help and treatment for himself, so that he would never sexually abuse anyone again.

They went to the Social Services Department and the people there said that if Ralph did not get treatment he might have to go to jail, because sexual abuse is wrong, and he could never do this again to Wanda or anyone. Ralph said that he felt _____ and _____ about what he had done, and that maybe he had a problem with wanting to give children bad touches because he had bad touches himself when he was young, and was sexually abused by his uncle. He was willing to go get treatment from a therapist so that he could stop his problem. And he understood that if he was not willing to change he would have to go to jail.

The Social Services Department said that Wanda might have to go to a foster home for a while until Ralph and her mother were able to work out a way to make sure that Wanda was never alone with him while he was getting treatment. A foster home is a special home where children live for a while when there are problems in their family. It made her very _____ and _____ to leave her mother, but her mother called every day, and came and visited her. Ralph kept going to see a counselor every week to get help for himself. But even after she came home, Wanda did not feel safe being alone with Ralph, and her mother never left them alone together. Wanda wished he would move someplace else, but her mother felt that Ralph could change and wanted him to live with them.

After all that had happened, and even though Ralph did not try to abuse her again, sometimes Wanda had bad dreams and felt _____ and _____ at night. She worried that someone would come in her room and give her a bad touch — maybe even Ralph. And she worried that people at school would know that she had had a bad touch on her private parts, and think she was a bad person. She even thought that people at school were talking about her, even though she knew that they really didn't know what had happened. Sometimes she would not even put on her gym clothes because she was _____ that people could look at her body and tell that her body had had a wrong, bad touch.

So Wanda went to the Social Services Department to see a counselor and to be in a group like this one. She learned what she should say if somebody tried to give her a wrong, bad touch. What should she say and do? _____
She learned that she should tell someone when something happened to her that made her feel _____ and _____. Whom should she tell? _____.
She learned to talk to herself when she started having _____ feelings. She learned to say:

I'm a good person, I'm proud of me.
I've been through a lot, but look how strong I've got!

She learned to talk to herself, and remind herself that what had happened to her was in the past, when she didn't know ways to get help. This is now, and she has learned ways to get help to keep from getting a wrong touch. She learned to say to herself:

That was then, but this is now!
I won't be abused and I know how!

Wanda had to talk to herself, and see a counselor, and be in a group. Now and then she has some bad feelings, but she does not feel very _____ or _____ anymore. She knows that abuse is not the child's fault, and that the adult should know better, and that the abuser must have bad problems.

She grew up and married a very nice man who never abused anyone. He had grown up in a nice, safe home and learned what was right and wrong, and he told Wanda when they had their own little girl, "You never have to worry about my giving our daughter a bad, wrong touch. Normal grown men give their sexual feelings to their wives, and give different kinds of love to their daughters and to children." Wanda trusted her husband, but she knew there were other people in the world with bad problems, so she taught her little girl Rachel about what she could do to keep from having wrong touches. She said, "Rachel, I am going to teach you about right and wrong touches, and I will teach you what to do if anyone ever tries to give you a wrong touch." And they both felt strong and _____, and said, "We know how to keep from being abused, and we know how to take care of ourselves, and who we can go to for help if we need it.

And Wanda and Rachel and her Daddy lived safely ever after.

MY OWN STORY
(Use With Session Seven)

Once upon a time there was a girl named _____ who lived in _____ with

_____. Her parents _____ (got along well, fussed, got along poorly and were

divorced, never saw each other, etc.). She knew a little bit about bad touches, because she had learned

some from _____ (school, TV, parents, other children), but she didn't know a lot about it.

Then one day _____ gave her a bad touch that was _____

(describe bad touch). This made her feel _____ (describe).

At first she didn't know what to do about it, because any time someone gives you a bad touch or

makes you give them a bad touch, you feel _____. She wasn't sure what to do or

whom to tell, and this made her feel _____. The reasons she thought it might be good

to tell someone were _____. The reasons she worried about telling

someone were _____. In some ways the person who abused

her was good to her because _____, but bad touches are sexual

abuse, and nobody has a right to do this to you. Children are too young to understand and handle sexual

touches and feelings. She did not understand why _____ gave her a bad touch, or why

anybody would do this to someone.

The way that the bad touches were found out was _____. After it

was all told, this is what happened _____

_____(what everybody did or didn't do about the bad touches). This is what

happened to her _____, and this is what happened to the person who sexu-

ally abused her _____. This is what happened to her family

_____.

When the sexual abuse was first told, she felt _____. At night when she was in

her bed, she had _____ thoughts, and sometimes she thought about _____

(what she thought would happen, fears that she had, worries that she had). Sometimes she even thought

that other people could tell she had been sexually abused just by looking at her, and this made her feel

_____ about herself. Sometimes she thought that people in her family like _____

were mad at her about the abuse, and maybe they blamed her for it, even though they really knew it was

not her fault. The thing that made her the most sad and mad about the abuse was _____

_____.

She talked to _____ about the abuse, and went to this group and learned how to talk about her feelings. She learned to remind herself that, "I'm a good person, I'm proud of _____ _____. I've been through a lot, but look how strong I've got."

Since she has talked to people and been in this special group, she knows more about what good and _____ touches are, and that bad touches are sexual abuse. She knows that sexual abuse is not the fault of the _____, and that normal adults know that they should not sexually abuse children, and that sexual abuse is against the _____. She knows now what to do if anybody else tries to give her a bad touch and abuses her. She knows that she can _____. Sometimes she is _____ that she did not know all these things when the bad touches and abuse first happened. At first she thought that she was different from other people, but now she knows that _____ people have been sexually abused, and that maybe even one out of every five girls in the United States has had bad touches and been sexually abused. She knows that people who sexually abuse children have bad problems inside themselves, and that they should get help for their problems, and that they will be punished if they keep on doing the abuse and not trying to change. She knows that she has learned lots of ways to keep sexual abuse from happening to her again, and that makes her feel more _____. She knows that sometimes bad things happen to good people and that she is a _____ person.

Someday when she grows up and gets married and maybe has a little girl of her own, she will teach her all about _____ and _____ touches, and will tell her ways to help take care of herself and get help from others, so that her little girl will be strong and know what to do about _____.

Moving On and Getting Stronger Game

ASSEMBLING THE GAME

1. To assemble the game board, photocopy pages E3 to E5 and tape the pages together (as shown below). If you wish, you can have this taped board copied to colored paper or card stock and laminated for durability and attractiveness. This can be done at any full service copy center, such as Kinko's.

Glue these pages together

So that they look like this

2. Checkers, round cardboard disks, or small party store objects (plastic Indians, cowboys, cars, etc.) can be used for the game pieces. Print each group member's name on small gummed labels and attach the names to the game pieces. You will need one die to roll to move the game pieces.
3. Both the *Moving On and Getting Stronger Game* and *The Life Game* (pp. I3-I5) use the same "Learning Cards." To prepare these cards, make double-sided photocopies on colored card stock with the "Learning Card" questions (pages J4-J8) on one side and the "Learning Card" icons (page J3) on the other. Then cut the copies on the dotted lines to make the two-sided cards.

DIRECTIONS FOR PLAY

"Learning Cards" are placed in a stack in the "Learning Card" space on the game board with questions face down. Players toss the die in turn and move their game pieces the number of spaces shown on the die. After moving the game piece, the player turns over the top "Learning Card," which is then answered or discussed with the group. After answering the question, the player returns the card to the bottom of the "Learning Card" pile. Some spaces have a ✳ icon; these are "Freebie" spaces. When the game piece lands on a "Freebie" space, the player can either answer a "Learning Card" question herself/himself or can choose another player in the group who must answer the question.

The object of the game is learning, by moving toward Mastery Mountain. The child who reaches the goal first may receive a small prize, such as a candy bar. It is unlikely that all questions will be covered in a single session, and leftovers may be used in the *TV Quiz Show Game* played in Session Fourteen (see pp. 81-82). It is also acceptable to repeat some questions in the *TV Quiz Show Game* if you cover more questions than expected during the game session.

Finish

Start

Freebie

M
Getti

SCARE

GUILTY GULL

FEEL BAD FOREST

MIXED-UP MOUNTAIN

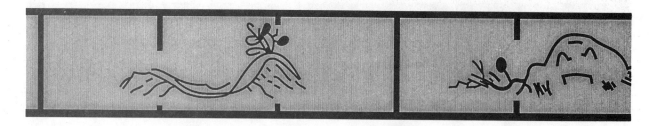

Moving On and
ng Stronger (

:D SWAMP

Freebie

UNDERST

Y

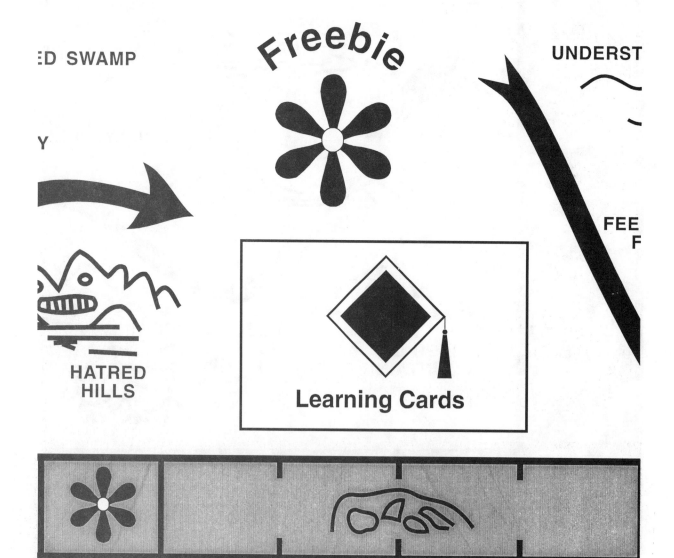

HATRED
HILLS

Learning Cards

FEE
F

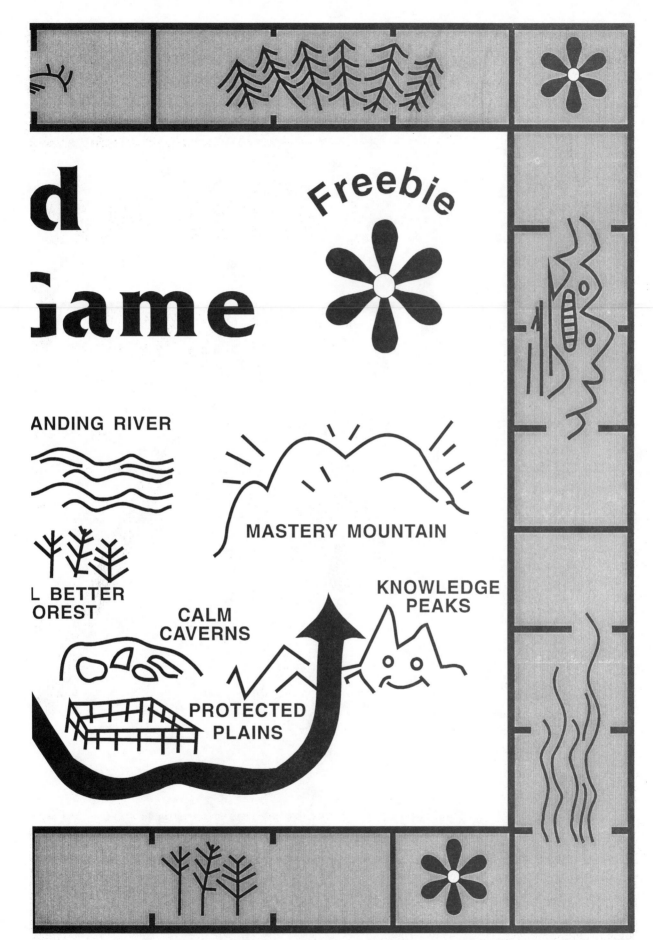

d

Game

Freebie

ANDING RIVER

MASTERY MOUNTAIN

L BETTER
OREST

CALM
CAVERNS

KNOWLEDGE
PEAKS

PROTECTED
PLAINS

Graduation Certificates

Certificate of Graduation

This certificate will show that _____ has successfully completed a Group Course called "Moving On and Getting Stronger." This certificate will show that the above person has learned facts about abuse, that she has learned that sometimes bad things happen to good people, and that it is not ever the child's fault. She has also learned what to do if someone tries to abuse her, and understands that we all have a right to keep our bodies private. _____ knows that she is a good person, and that she has a right to be proud of herself. If something happens in the future, _____ can contact the group leaders or social worker at the following phone number: _____. The above-named person also knows how to call the police at 911. She has learned that she is a strong person, and a good person. What happened was THEN; this is NOW. _____ knows what to do to keep from being abused.

CONGRATULATIONS!

Signed _____ Date _____

F3

Certificate of Graduation

This certificate will show that _____ has successfully completed a Group Course called "Moving On and Getting Stronger." This certificate will show that the above person has learned facts about abuse, that he has learned that sometimes bad things happen to good people, and that it is not ever the child's fault. He has also learned what to do if someone tries to abuse him, and understands that we all have a right to keep our bodies private. _____ knows that he is a good person, and that he has a right to be proud of himself. If something happens in the future, _____ can contact the group leaders or social worker at the following phone number: _____. The above-named person also knows how to call the police at 911. He has learned that he is a strong person, and a good person. What happened was THEN; this is NOW. _____ knows what to do to keep from being abused.

CONGRATULATIONS!

Signed _____   Date _____

F4

My Own

That Was Then, But This Is Now

Activity Book

Name: _____

My Three Wishes

1. _____
   _____
   _____

2. _____
   _____
   _____

3. _____
   _____
   _____

**Add any others you would like to remember
from the list made in group:**

_____
_____
_____
_____
_____
_____
_____
_____
_____

Three Things I Need
Band-Aids For

1. _____
   _____
   _____

2. _____
   _____
   _____

3. _____
   _____
   _____

List any other "hurts" you wanted to remember from the list made in group:

_____
_____
_____
_____
_____
_____
_____
_____

Things I Want to
Work On the Most

_____

_____

_____

_____

_____

_____

_____

_____

_____

_____

_____

_____

_____

_____

_____

_____

_____

_____

Rules We Use in
This Group

1. _____
_____
_____

2. _____
_____
_____

3. _____
_____
_____

4. _____
_____
_____

5. _____
_____
_____

6. _____
_____

7. _____
_____
_____

The Things I Would Like to See Added to the "Wouldn't It Be Nice" Coloring Book

"Mirror, Mirror on the Wall"

**Questions I would really like answered
about me and the abuse that happened to me:**

_____

_____

_____

_____

_____

_____

_____

_____

_____

_____

_____

_____

_____

_____

_____

_____

_____

_____

_____

_____

_____

_____

A Letter to the Person Who Sexually Abused Me

Date: _____

To: _____

From: _____

_____

_____

_____

_____

_____

_____

_____

_____

_____

_____

_____

_____

_____

_____

_____

_____

_____

_____

_____

_____

G9

Ten Good Things About Me

1. _____

_____

2. _____

_____

3. _____

_____

4. _____

_____

5. _____

_____

6. _____

_____

7. _____

_____

8. _____

_____

9. _____

_____

10. _____

_____

Three Ways Abuse Made Me
Feel Bad About Myself

1. _____
   _____
   _____

2. _____
   _____
   _____

3. _____
   _____
   _____

What I can expect to change about me:

_____
_____
_____
_____
_____
_____
_____
_____

Rules for Negotiation

1. Know exactly what actions you want from the other person or specifically what you would like him or her to do.

2. Be able to communicate those actions to the other person in a clear, polite manner.

3. Be able to give clear, adequate reasons WHY you want or need something from the other person.

4. Suggest some solutions to any problems you expect the other person might have in doing this for you.

5. Explain and apologize for any misunderstanding or confusion in the past that has prevented this person from doing what you are asking of him or her.

6. Offer something to the other person in return for his or her cooperation.

7. Be ready to suggest some compromise or alternative solution.

8. Express appreciation for any change or compromise from the other person.

Rules for Negotiating

(Copy from board or attach a copy to your booklet)

1. _____

_____

2. _____

_____

3. _____

_____

4. _____

_____

5. _____

_____

6. _____

_____

7. _____

_____

8. _____

_____

Notes About Relaxation

My visualization "scene" for relaxing:

_____

_____

_____

_____

_____

_____

_____

_____

**My "mantra" for relaxing
(word or phrase I say to myself):**

_____

_____

_____

_____

_____

_____

_____

_____

What I Will Teach
My Grandaughter (Grandson)

_____

(Fill in her [his] name)

_____

_____

_____

_____

_____

_____

_____

_____

_____

_____

_____

_____

_____

_____

_____

_____

_____

The Things I Need to Continue to Work on Are

_____

_____

_____

_____

_____

_____

_____

_____

_____

_____

_____

_____

_____

_____

_____

_____

_____

_____

_____

The Things I Would Like to See Included in These Groups in the Future Are

_____

_____

_____

_____

_____

_____

_____

_____

_____

_____

_____

_____

_____

_____

_____

_____

_____

_____

A Special Note for You
From _____

You have graduated. Congratulations!

_____

_____

_____

_____

_____

_____

_____

If you ever need to contact me, here is how:

_____

_____

_____

_____

_____

_____

_____

Homework Assignments
For Ages 13 to 16

HOMEWORK ASSIGNMENT #1
(Assign With Session Two)

Tell your mother (caretaker) about the three wishes you made in group. Ask her (him) if she (he) would have made the same three wishes. Ask her (him) to make up three wishes of her (his) own and write them down here. Then tell her (him) about the ways we are going to work on your three wishes in the group: How we can't make them come true, but we are going to help you understand those feelings, learn to deal with those feelings, and learn ways to keep yourself safe so you won't be abused again.

Your mother's (caretaker's) three wishes:

1. _____

2. _____

3. _____

HOMEWORK ASSIGNMENT #2
(Assign With Session Three)

Tell your mother (caretaker) about the coloring book that we reviewed in the group. Ask her (him) what she (he) thought was the most important thing people would put in a book for young children about sexual abuse, and why. Write her (his) answer below. Did you agree? What did *you* think was the most important thing?

What my mother (caretaker) thinks should be in a book about sexual abuse for young children:

_____

_____

_____

What I think should be in the book:

_____

_____

_____

HOMEWORK ASSIGNMENT #3
(Assign With Session Four)

Tell your mother (caretaker) about the "myths" or mistakes in people's thinking about sexual abuse that we talked about in the group. Ask her (him) what she (he) thinks the biggest mistake people make in their thinking about sexual abuse. Ask her (him) what was the biggest thing she (he) didn't understand about sexual abuse before it happened in your family. Write down her (his) answers. Tell her (him) what *you* thought was the biggest mistake people make in their thinking about sexual abuse.

What my mother (caretaker) thought was the biggest "myth" about sexual abuse:

_____

_____

_____

What my mother (caretaker) didn't understand about sexual abuse before it happened in our family:

_____

_____

_____

What I think is the biggest "myth":

_____

_____

_____

HOMEWORK ASSIGNMENT #4
(Assign With Session Five)

Think of a question about sexual abuse or about your family's feelings that you have not asked your mother (caretaker) before. Ask her (him) if it is okay to ask a question that you have wondered about, then write down your question and her (his) answer below.

My question:

_____

_____

My mother's (caretaker's) answer:

_____

_____

_____

HOMEWORK ASSIGNMENT #5
(Assign With Session Six)

Tell your mother (caretaker) about some of the ways we talked about to take care of yourself in the future, so that you won't be sexually abused again. Ask her (him) if she (he) has any other ideas about how you or anyone can keep themselves safe from abuse. If she (he) can think of some ways like ones we mentioned in the group, write them down. Tell her (him) about one of the situations we talked about in the group, and ask her (him) what she (he) thought she (he) might have done when she (he) was your age if that had happened to her (him). Write down her (his) answer.

Ways my mother (caretaker) thinks someone can keep herself (himself) safe from sexual abuse:

_____

_____

_____

What my mother (caretaker) thinks she (he) would have done if she (he) were my age:

_____

_____

_____

HOMEWORK ASSIGNMENT #6
(Assign With Session Seven)

Ask your mother (caretaker) what she (he) would like to see you be like when you are 21 years old, and write down her (his) answer. Is it different from yours? Ask her (him) to imagine she (he) goes with you to see the abuser when you are 21 years old. What would she (he) like to say to the abuser? Write down her (his) answer.

What my mother (caretaker) would like to say about me when I am 21:

_____

_____

_____

What my mother (caretaker) would like to say to the abuser if she (he) went with me to see the abuser when I am 21:

_____

_____

_____

HOMEWORK ASSIGNMENT #7
(Assign With Session Eight)

Ask your mother (caretaker) to name three things she (he) likes about you. Write them down. Then you name three things you like about her (him) and write them down.

What my mother (caretaker) likes about me:

1. _____

2. _____

3. _____

What I like about my mother (caretaker):

1. _____

2. _____

3. _____

HOMEWORK ASSIGNMENT #8
(Assign With Session Nine)

Take home a copy of your negotiation outline. Pick something your mother (caretaker) would like to negotiate on. Make it really simple, like what day you do certain chores, or when you want to buy an outfit she (he) doesn't like, or wear some of her (his) clothes to school. Then go through the negotiation steps.

Step 1. What I want:

_____

_____

Step 2. Clear communication (state what you want very clearly):

_____

_____

Step 3. Reasons I want this:

_____

_____

Step 4. Solutions I have to why she (he) might have a problem with it:

_____

_____

Step 5. Explanations and apologies for misunderstandings in the past:

_____

_____

Step 6. What I can offer her (him) in return for her (his) cooperation:

_____

_____

Step 7. My compromise or alternative suggestion:

_____

_____

Step 8. My expression of appreciation to her (him):

_____

_____

RESULTS:

_____

_____

_____

HOMEWORK ASSIGNMENT #9
(Assign With Session Ten)

Practice all the relaxation steps we learned in group at least twice during the week. Write down what you found to be the hardest part to do.

_____

_____

_____

_____

_____

HOMEWORK ASSIGNMENT #10
(Assign With Session Eleven)

Make a list of the ways that you think you have gotten stronger since you have been in this group. Do you think you are less afraid you will be abused again? Do you think that some of the things you learned will help you in other situations (like when you are feeling nervous, or when you need to negotiate something with someone)?

Ways I have gotten stronger:

_____

_____

_____

_____

Am I afraid I will be abused again? _____

Will I use my learning from the group in other situations? _____

_____

_____

When? _____

_____

_____

The Life Game

ASSEMBLING THE GAME

1. To assemble the game board for *The Life Game*, photocopy pages I3 to I5 and tape the pages together (as shown below). If you wish, you can have this taped board copied to colored paper or card stock and laminated for durability and attractiveness. This can be done at any full service copy center, such as Kinko's.

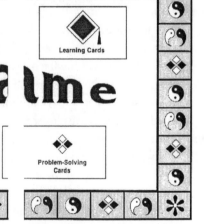

Glue these pages together

So that they look like this

2. Checkers, round cardboard disks, or small party store objects (plastic Indians, cowboys, cars, etc.) can be used for the game pieces. Print each group member's name on small gummed labels and attach the names to the game pieces. You will need one die to roll to move the game pieces.

3. Both *The Life Game* and *The Moving On and Getting Stronger Game* (pp. E3-E5) use the same "Learning Cards"; however, *The Life Game* also uses other cards ("Knowing Yourself," "Understanding Each Other," and "Problem-Solving") that focus specifically on the developmental tasks of adolescence. To prepare these cards, make double-sided photocopies on colored card stock with the "Learning Card" questions (pages J4-J8) on one side and the "Learning Card" icons (page J3) on the other. Then cut the copies on the dotted lines to make the two-sided cards. Make the "Understanding Each Other Cards" (pages J9 to J15), "Knowing Yourself Cards" (pages J16 to J22), and "Problem-Solving Cards" (pages J23 to J28) the same way (photocopies with appropriate questions on one side and appropriate icon on the other side).

DIRECTIONS FOR PLAY

"Learning Cards," "Knowing Yourself Cards," "Understanding Each Other Cards," and "Problem-Solving Cards" are placed in stacks in the appropriate spaces on the game board with questions down. Players toss the die in turn and move their game pieces the number of spaces shown on the die. Most spaces have an icon indicating the question category to be used. Some spaces have a ✱ icon; these are "Freebie" spaces. Each time a 1 or 2 is rolled on the die, the player moves her/his game piece the corresponding number of spaces and reads the question on the top card in the pile of "Learning Cards" and then answers that question. After answering the question, the player returns the card to the bottom of the "Learning Card" pile. When the game piece lands on a "Freebie" space, the player can either answer the "Learning Card" question herself/himself or can choose another player in the group who must answer the question. When a 3, 4, 5, or 6 is rolled on the die, the player moves the game piece the number of spaces shown, reads the question on the top card in the pile matching the game board icon ("Knowing Yourself," "Understanding Each Other," or "Problem-Solving"), and answers that question.

This game facilitates group activity. The object of the game is NOT to "finish" the game. Instead, use the game to try to spend as much time as possible on group discussion of each question.

This game has been used in a number of different types of structured adolescent groups, and is appropriate for groups focusing on many types of social skills building. The inclusion of the "Learning Cards" makes the game specific to groups for sexually abused adolescents. "Knowing Yourself," "Problem-Solving," and "Understanding Each Other" cards have been developed to deal with many aspects of the developmental tasks of adolescence. Some of their questions are aimed at mixed-gender groups, and therapists may wish to exclude or explain these.

Questions in each card category (except "Learning Cards") have been experimentally rated for degree of difficulty and level of intimacy required. The letters and numbers printed in the lower right hand corner of each card indicate that card's levels of difficulty and intimacy. Difficulty is rated from "A" = easy to "E" = difficult. Intimacy is rated from "1" = lowest level of intimacy to "20" = highest level of intimacy. *(Note: Some card categories have maximum levels of intimacy lower than 20.)* Therapists may want to use these ratings to "stack the deck" so that the cards on top of the pile are appropriate for the functional level of the group and/or emphasize subjects the group is likely to be discussing.

Finish

Start

Freebie

The

Knowing Yourself
Cards

Life Ga

**Understanding Each
Other Cards**

Learning Cards

lme

Problem-Solving
Cards

Game Cards

Learning Cards

Learning Cards

Learning Cards

Learning Cards

Learning Cards

Learning Cards

Learning Cards

Learning Cards

Learning Cards

What is a bad touch? Give an example of a bad touch. Ask the people on your left and right to tell you an example of a bad touch. What is an example of a bad touch somebody might ask you to give?

What is the first thing you should do if someone tries to give you a bad touch and sexually abuse you? Ask the people on your left and right to say what they would do.

What if the first person you told did nothing to stop the abuse? Who should you tell then? Ask the people on your left and right to say who they would tell.

What is sexual abuse? Have the people on your left and right give examples of sexual abuse.

Who is the first person you would tell if someone tried to give you a bad touch or sexually abuse you? Ask the people on your left and right to answer the same question.

How many people should you tell about the abuse? Ask the people on your left and right to help you answer this question.

What is a bad secret that you should not keep? Have the people on your left and right give an example of a bad secret and a good secret.

Who is the first person you would tell if someone tried to give you a bad touch. Ask the people on your left and right to answer the question also.

If nobody you tell stops the abuse, what else could you do to stop it? Ask the people on your left and right to help you answer the question.

What kinds of help can a sexual abuser get to change himself (herself)? Have the people on your left and right help you with the question.

Is there anything a child does which makes the abuser want to abuse her (him)? Is it the child's fault? Have the people on your left and right answer these questions.

Is sexual abuse the child's fault if she (he) doesn't tell someone the first time the abuse happens? Have the people on your left and right answer the question also.

Why does a person lie about sexually abusing a child? Why don't they tell the truth? Have the people on your left and right help you answer these questions.

Can a sexual abuser get away with lying about sexual abuse? Have the people on your left and right help you with your answer.

What makes an adult or older person want to sexually abuse children? Have the people on your left and right help you with the question.

Why is sexual abuse against the law? Ask the people on your left and right to answer the question.

Does an adult, even a parent, have the right to give a child bad touches or sexually abuse children? Ask the people on your left and right to answer this question also.

What kinds of things can happen to an adult or other person who sexually abuses a child? Have the people on your left and right answer the question also.

How many people get sexually abused in the United States? Have the people on your left and right answer the question also.

Name some famous people who have told about being sexually abused when they were children. Have the people on your left and right help you with the answer.

Can someone tell just by looking at a person that she (he) has been sexually abused? Have the people on your left and right answer the question also.

Why do mothers (caretakers) sometimes seem to be angry with their children for telling about the abuse? Have the people on your left and right answer the question also.

What sometimes happens in families when a child tells about sexual abuse, and the Social Services Department becomes involved? Have the people on your left and right help you answer the question.

Why are some children who are sexually abused sent to live in foster homes for a while after the abuse is known? Have the people on your left and right answer the question also.

What are some reasons a child does not tell about the abuse right away? Have the people on your left and right answer the question with you.

What are some of the ways a sexual abuser gets the child to go along with the abuse? Have the people on your left and right help you with the answer.

Why would a mother (caretaker) have trouble believing a child who told her (him) about sexual abuse by somebody in the family or a close friend? Have the people on your left and right help answer the question.

Some people think that when they are older their husbands (wives) or boyfriends (girlfriends) will like them less because they have been abused. Is this true? Have the people on your left and right discuss this with you.

Lots of people feel two ways about the person who abused them. They like some things about them and hate some things. Tell two ways you felt about the person who abused you, and have the people on your left and right answer the same question.

What would you like to say to the person who abused you? Have the people on your left and right answer the same question.

Do other people who don't understand about abuse sometimes blame the child? Have the people on your left and right answer the same question.

Do family members (brothers, sisters, uncles, etc.) sometimes act angry toward the child who tells about sexual abuse? Have the people on your left and right tell why they think this happens.

Do some children feel like they are different from other children in some way and that is the reason they were abused? Have the people on your left and right answer this question.

Name some feelings that people sometimes have about themselves after they have been abused. Have the people on your left and right help with the answer.

What are some of the effects that sexual abuse sometimes has on a person who has been abused? Have the people on your left and right answer also.

What kind of help can a child receive who has been sexually abused? Where can she (he) receive it? Have the people on your left and right help with the answers.

Name three strong and good things about yourself and have the people on your left and right tell three strong and good things about themselves.

Tell what you would do to help keep yourself from being sexually abused again. Have the people on your left and right answer the same question.

What are you going to teach your own children about sexual abuse? Have the people on your left and right answer the same question.

How can you keep reminding yourself that you are a good person and that abuse is not your fault? Ask the people on your left and right to answer the same question.

**Understanding Each
Other Cards**

**Understanding Each
Other Cards**

**Understanding Each
Other Cards**

**Understanding Each
Other Cards**

**Understanding Each
Other Cards**

**Understanding Each
Other Cards**

**Understanding Each
Other Cards**

**Understanding Each
Other Cards**

**Understanding Each
Other Cards**

A7

What kinds of things should the therapist or group leader be allowed to tell your parents about what she or he learns about the group? What responsibilities does the group leader have to your parents?

B1

Tell what you think is the most important thing a person can teach a child. Have two other people in the group list what they think is the most important.

B2

Tell which person in your family you feel furthest from, and why. Pick two other people in the group to answer this question.

A4

Pick two people in the group and tell something about them you would like to copy.

A5

Explain to the group some of the reasons why you are here in the group and ask each member to do the same.

A6

Add to any rules the group has made, and help the group make a list of rules that will be used in all your sessions. Have the whole group participate, and have someone write down the rules.

A1

Ask each person in the group to tell something you did not know about them. Do not ask anything too personal. Have the person on your left do the same thing.

A2

Do you think it is important to say nice things to people you like? How often and in what ways do you think it should be done?

A3

Act out: Stand in front of each person in the group and tell her or him something you like about the way she or he looks or acts. Pick one other person to go around and do the same.

What is the most recent compliment you have given someone else? Is it hard for you to give compliments? When and how do you usually give them?

B9

All the girls in the neighborhood but one were invited to a slumber party. Why would this probably happen? How would she feel, and what would she probably do? Have a person of the opposite sex answer this question also.

C1

If you have a bad reputation and decide to change, how can you get across to people that you are different now? Have the person on your right answer, also.

C2

What kinds of things is a parent supposed to do for you? What do you expect them to do for you? What do they *not* do for you that they should, and what do they do you think they shouldn't? Ask the same question to the person on your left.

B6

How can you tell when a person's feelings are really hurt? What do you usually do when your feelings are hurt? Ask the person on your left to tell what she or he does when feelings get hurt? Show the expression and posture of hurt feelings.

B7

A boy or girl (opposite sex from you) whom you don't especially like keeps hanging around and asking for dates, and so on. How do you let her/him know you don't want to date or be friends without hurting feelings?

B8

Does the way a person acts on the outside always show how she or he feels on the inside? Give examples using yourself and something you have done and felt.

B3

Tell what kinds of clothes you usually wear. Describe your usual outfit. What do you want those clothes to say about you? To boys? To girls? Ask a group member of the opposite sex this same question.

B4

When you really dislike someone, how do you usually act around her or him? Has this made problems for you in the past? Ask the people on your right and left to answer these questions.

B5

Think of someone you do not like. Without saying his or her name, tell the things he or she does that make you dislike the person. Ask the person directly across from you to do the same thing.

C3

Do you think it is okay to use dirty words? When? What rules do you think people should go by in using dirty words? Are they different for boys than girls? Does it depend on the situation? Explain your ideas and ask a person of the opposite sex to explain.

C6

Pretend you are writing a "want ad" in the school paper for a friend of the opposite sex. What would you ask for? Discuss this with the group.

C9

If someone is not handsome or pretty, can he or she still be happy and popular? What do they have to do?

C4

Did you ever do something just because you wanted to spite someone who was pushing really hard to get you to do the opposite thing (like date someone your parents hated even though you didn't like him or her very much)?

C7

What is the most recent criticism someone gave you? Who gave it and what did you feel about it? What did you do as a result of it?

C10

Pretend you are writing a "want ad" for the school paper for a friend (same sex). What would you ask for in a friend? Would you "hire" yourself for a friend using the requirements in the ad? Discuss with the group.

C5

What's the difference in loving somebody and being sexually attracted to them? Have someone in the group (of the opposite sex) answer the question after you do.

C8

What rights do you think parents have in expecting things from their children (like the way you behave, the decisions you make, and so on)? What will you expect from your own children? Have the group make a list of "Parents' Rights."

C11

Who in your life now are you most likely to lose your temper with? Ask the person on your right the same question.

C12

Most teenagers are hurt by their parents getting a divorce. How do they sometimes "get back" at their parents? How do they hurt their parents to get even?

C15

Who (in this group) tries to be the most helpful to others in the group? Does the person on your right agree with your choice?

C18

Who seems the most at ease in this group? Ask a person of the opposite sex if he or she agrees with your choice.

C13

What do some of your friends do that you think is rude? What do you do the most that some other people have said is rude? Ask the person on your right the same questions.

C16

Who in this group does everyone think is the quietest? Ask a person of the opposite sex if he or she agrees with your choice.

C19

Tell each member of the group what you imagine it would take to make her or him happy and why.

C14

A foreign student is assigned to live with your family. What would he or she go home and tell his or her countrymen about your family? How would he or she describe the people in it, how they act, what their problems are, what they worry about, and so on?

C17

Tell about one time when you felt left out of a group. What did you do about it? What do you think makes people leave others out of a group? Have the people on your right and left answer the same questions.

C20

If you were the leader of this group, who would you worry about the most and why? Does the leader agree with your choice?

D1

Who has the most trouble telling their feelings in this group? What ideas do you have about how the group can help her or him? Does the person on your right agree?

D4

What kinds of things do people do in everyday life that really disgust you (picking teeth, using dirty words, and so on)? Have three other group members answer the question.

D7

Name some of the reasons parents do not trust their teenagers. What would make you trust or distrust your teenager if you were a parent? (Have a person of the opposite sex answer these questions also.)

D2

Who seems the most nervous in this group? Do you have any ideas about how to make her or him more comfortable in group? Ask the person on your right to answer these questions also.

D5

Who usually seems the most worried in the group? Is there some way the group can help make this person more comfortable? Ask the person on your right to help answer these questions.

D8

Say something mean you would like to say to your parents, a friend, and a teacher, but are afraid to. Why can't you say it to them? Why do you think you should keep that thought inside? Are there times when people really *should* keep their thoughts inside? Discuss with the group.

D3

Who in this group seems angriest most of the time? Ask a person of the opposite sex if he or she agrees with your choice. Do you think the group can help this person with his or her feelings? How?

D6

Who bosses people around sometimes in this group? Ask the group leader to comment on your choice.

D9

Do you think that even your own parents hate you sometimes? How do they usually act when you think they may be feeling that way? What have you usually done which seems to cause it? Ask the person on your right to answer the same questions.

E4

Act out: You bring a friend home and your parents are drunk. (Assign group members to be parents and friend.) Show how you would act. Then talk about how you handled your feelings. Discuss with the group.

E1

Do you know anyone who committed or attempted suicide? Why do you think people do this? What do you think about them? Ask the person on your right the same question.

E2

Have you ever wished, even for a little while, that someone you really liked most of the time, was dead? Do you think most people have this kind of thought sometimes? Ask three people on your left the same questions.

E3

Tell the person sitting on your right and the person sitting on your left anything they have done or said in group that you did not agree with. Why was it hard for you to tell them at the time they did or said it?

D10

What is the most frequent criticism that you get from other people? Why do you think they say it? Have the person on your right tell why they think people might say that about you. Then have two others answer this question about themselves.

D11

What is a homosexual? What makes people become homosexual? How can you tell if somebody is homosexual? How do you feel about them? Lead the group in a discussion of this question.

D12

Knowing Yourself Cards

Knowing Yourself Cards

Knowing Yourself Cards

Knowing Yourself Cards

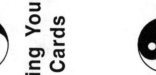

Knowing Yourself Cards

Knowing Yourself Cards

Knowing Yourself Cards

Knowing Yourself Cards

Knowing Yourself Cards

If you could change into a movie star, who would you pick and why? Ask the person on your right the same question.

A7

If you could only get one thing for Christmas or your birthday, what would you pick? Ask the person on your left the same question.

A8

What are some of the nicknames you have had? What did you feel about them? Pick another person to answer these questions also.

B1

If you could wish for a talent, what would it be? Ask one other person this question.

A4

If you were on a desert island and could take only one person with you, who would you take and why?

A5

If your house were on fire and all the people and pets were out, and you could carry only two things out for yourself, what would you carry?

A6

If you were on a desert island and could take only three things with you, what would you take and why? Ask the person on your left the same question.

A1

What animal would you like to be? Why? Ask another person these questions.

A2

What is the best and worst thing about the school you go to?

A3

B8

When you daydream about things you would like to be or do, what do you think about? Ask the person on your left this question, too. Do you think these dreams will ever come true? If not, why not?

B9

Act out: Pretend you have to give a short speech at a banquet under this situation: You have been picked as the most improved player on the boys'/girls' basketball team.

B10

Name the person in your school you would most like to be like. What do you like about that person (looks and personality)?

B5

What have you done that you are the most proud of? Have the people on your left and right answer the question also.

B6

Act this out: Pretend you have to give a short speech at a banquet under this situation: You have been elected the most-liked girl/boy in your class. Thank the group.

B7

What is the thing you did in the past year that you enjoyed the most? Why? Have the person on your left also answer these questions.

B2

Did you ever have a pet you really loved? What happened to it? Tell what you liked about it and why it was important to you.

B3

Tell the things about you that are like your mother (caretaker), and the things that are like your father (caretaker). Have the person on your right do the same thing.

B4

What was the last compliment you got? What did you think about it?

C5

How can a person tell if he or she is in love? After you answer, have someone in the group of the opposite sex answer.

C6

How long should you expect love to last between a boy and a girl? Have a person in the group of the opposite sex answer the same question.

C7

Without using words, show the person across from you that you are sad. Have him or her do the same thing.

C2

What are the things you want the most in a person you would go steady with? Ask the people on your right and left to answer the question.

C3

What do you think you will be like 10 years from now? What job, what family, what lifestyle? Is it different from what you would really want? Ask three other people the same questions.

C4

Tell which person in your family you feel closest to and why. Pick two other people in the group to answer the same question.

B11

How do you usually act at a party? What kinds of parties are you most comfortable with? Ask two other people the same questions.

B12

What do you think should decide whether people should get married or not? How will you decide whether to get married? Ask the person of the opposite sex nearest to you on the right the same questions.

C1

What is the thing you did in the past year that you hated the most? Why? Ask the people on your left and right the same questions.

What is the most recent criticism that you gave about someone else? Tell about it. Is it hard for you to criticize someone? When and how do you usually do it?

C8

What kinds of things do your parents argue about? Is it usually one person's fault? How do you think you will handle things like that when you're married? Ask a person of the opposite sex the same questions.

D3

What do you think is the most unfair thing that ever happened to you? Did you do anything to make it happen? Have two other people answer these questions.

D6

Tell about a mistake you once made. How would you do it differently now? What made you make that mistake? Pick one other person and ask the same questions.

D1

Do you think it is normal to hate people sometimes that you really love most of the time? How do you usually handle these feelings if you have them? Ask the people on your left and right.

D4

When do you think people should seriously think about running away from home? When do you think it could be the right thing to do? What could happen that might be worse than staying home? What other things could a person do instead of running away?

D7

How does your body feel inside when you have something to tell the group but are scared to say it? What do you usually do? Have the person on your right answer the same questions.

D2

Tell about a time that you gave up on something you really wanted to do. How did it make you feel, and what happened? What kinds of things make you want to give up? Ask the person on your right the same questions.

D5

How does your body feel inside when someone asks you a really personal question you don't want to answer? What do you usually do?

D8

Have you ever cheated on some-thing? Why do you think you did it? Is there anything else you could have done? Ask the people on your left and right to answer.

E2

Think of the saddest thing that ever happened to you. Was there anything you could do to keep it from happening? How did you handle your feelings? Have the people on your left and right an-swer.

E3

What kinds of things do you think you would most likely lie about or try to hide about yourself? What have you lied or hidden in the past? Ask the person on your right the same questions.

E4

What is the most scared you have ever been? What did you do? How do you usually handle scared feel-ings? Have the person on your right answer the same questions.

D12

Act out a scene about a time re-cently when your feelings got hurt. Assign parts to different group members, and tell them what to say. Have each member tell how she or he felt about what the char-acter might have been thinking. The leader will help you.   **D13**

Tell about the last time you cried. What upset you? What kinds of things usually make you cry? Ask the people on your left and right to answer these questions also.

E1

Do you feel someone was cruel to you sometime this month? Think of a time. How did you feel? What do you think made him or her do it? Have the person on your right answer these questions.

D9

Tell about a time when you felt really lonely. What did you do about it? How do you usually handle your lonely feelings? Have a person on your right (of the op-posite sex) answer the same ques-tions.   **D10**

If you could change only one cer-tain thing you have done in your life so far, what would you pick? Ask the people on your left and right the same question.

D11

Have you ever deliberately tried to hurt yourself? Have you thought about doing it? What was going on, and what did you finally do? Ask the person on your right the same questions.

E5

What is the meanest thing you ever did to someone else? What made you do it? How would you handle it differently now? Have the person on your right answer the same questions.

E6

How do you usually handle your really sexy feelings? What do you believe are the normal ways that most teenagers handle their sexual feelings?

E7

Problem-Solving Cards

 Problem-Solving Cards

 Problem-Solving Cards

 **Problem-Solving Cards**

Problem-Solving Cards

Problem-Solving Cards

 **Problem-Solving Cards**

 Problem-Solving Cards

 Problem-Solving Cards

J23

A1

If your grades were really bad, and a big exam was coming up which would make you pass or fail, *and* you had the chance that night to go to a big concert you liked, what would you do and why? Ask the person on your left the same question.

A2

Should you tell other people outside the group that you come to group therapy or have therapy of any kind? Ask each member of the group what she or he plans to do about this.

A3

When, if ever, do you think a person can lie to his or her parents? What usually happens when you do this?

A4

Act out: Your teacher tells you that you have failed a grade. Act out what you would say and do. Then tell how you would feel and how you would handle your feelings later. Have the group leader assign the teacher's part, then you lead the group discussion afterwards.

B1

Act out how you act when you meet a new girl and a new boy. Have people on your left and right help you, while you play yourself. Ask them if you seemed nervous or relaxed, and how they knew.

B2

What kinds of things happening in the group make it hard to enjoy? Does it ever get too noisy, too silly? What can be done when things seem to be going badly?

B3

You didn't make the basketball team, although you tried very hard. Act out what you would do when the coach told you (leader plays the coach). Tell what you would do later to handle your disappointment.

B4

How do you think teenagers should be punished by parents? What do you think is fair? Tell about a fair and unfair punishment you have had from your parents. Have each member do the same.

B5

Have you heard of teenagers who use their parents' divorce to get things they want? What kinds of things do they get?

Act out how you will act when you are a parent with teenagers. Have the leader assign roles. Pretend your teen brings home a terrible report card. Tell if the way you react is different from what your parents would do.

B9

Suppose you knew your 13-year-old sister was thinking about having sex with someone. What would you tell her? What would you do? Have a person of the opposite sex answer these questions.

C3

Act out: Persuade the person on your left to do something that will probably get you both into trouble (drugs, cheating, and so on). Then let the person decide what he or she would do in this situation. Tell how each of you felt, and ask the group how you could have handled it differently.

C1

FOR GIRLS ONLY: IF YOU ARE A BOY, PASS THIS TO THE GIRL ON YOUR LEFT. A boy makes a pass at you on the first date, and you don't like this. What will you probably do and say?

C4

Suppose your friend hurt your feelings without seeming to know it. What would you do? Ask the person on your left.

C2

Your mother (caretaker) snoops in your room. Why do you think a mother (caretaker) would do this, and what could a teenager do about it?

C5

You didn't get elected cheerleader although you thought you should. Act out what you would do when told you didn't make it. Then tell how you felt inside, and how you handled your disappointment. (Leader can assign roles.)

B6

Your 13-year-old sister plans to run away from home because your mother (caretaker) put her on restriction. What would you tell her? Have a person of the opposite sex answer this question also.

B7

Act out a time you handled your angry feelings well. A time you handled them poorly. Assign the parts needed to other group members, and have the group discuss the differences in your behavior between the two scenes.

B8

J25

Act out: You are working at McDonald's and the manager yells at you about your work in front of everyone. Assign the roles, and show how you would probably react. Discuss the ways you usually handle situations like this, and tell how you felt during the scene.

C12

Your mother (caretaker) won't let you go to the beach with friends. Act out the argument, with the person on your left being one of your parents. Show what you would do, then act out one other way of handling it. Discuss with the group.

C13

Act out: A teacher accuses you of cheating (you didn't). Have the person on your left be the teacher, and show how you'd react. Then show another way to handle your anger. Discuss with the group.

C14

Why do you think a girl might get pregnant even when she really does not want to have a baby? Have the group make a list of the most common reasons.

C9

If a mother (caretaker) works, what should be the responsibilities of teenagers in helping with housework? If she (he) doesn't work? Lead the group in a discussion of this.

C10

Act out: Pretend you are breaking up with your boyfriend or girlfriend. Show how you think this could be done so everyone would not be hurt. (Leader assigns parts.)

C11

FOR BOYS ONLY: IF YOU'RE A GIRL, GIVE THIS TO THE BOY ON YOUR RIGHT. A girl acts flirty and sexy and leads you to think she would like to have sex, but then acts insulted if you try petting or sex. What would you say and do? Why do you think girls do this?

C6

If you were the leader of this group, what would you do differently?

C7

Suppose your mother and father are divorced. The one you live with keeps saying ugly things about the other. How would you handle this?

C8

Do certain people you know get picked on more than others? What do they seem to get picked on for? Do you think they bring it on themselves, or they can't stand up for themselves? Discuss with the group.

C15

You applied for a part-time Christmas job at a department store, and the manager told you that you didn't get it. How would you handle your feelings of disappointment?

C18

What do you think teenagers should know about birth control? Where do you think this information should be learned and offered?

D3

You find out that your boyfriend (girlfriend) has secretly been dating your cousin. Act out what you would do. (Leader assigns roles of cousin and friend.) Tell how else you might handle your feelings.

C16

What rules do you think a girl (boy) should have about having sex? (Have the boys make up a list and the girls make up a list.)

D1

Have you ever been afraid you were becoming an alcoholic? How can a person know when his or her drinking is really serious? Discuss this with the group.

D4

You argue with your parents (caretaker) over a person (of the same sex) you choose as a friend. (Leader assigns roles.) Act out the scene and discuss with the group.

C17

You don't want to take any kinds of drugs, but your date wants you to smoke pot. You don't want to, but you like your new boyfriend (girlfriend). How would you handle it. Ask a person of the opposite sex the same question.

D2

A friend who has lots of money and a fancy house comes home with you to your house, which is not very clean or nice. How would you act and handle your feelings? Act it out with a person next to you if it is too hard to say in words.

D5

J27

Suppose you were scared that you were hooked on drugs or pills. What kinds of help can you get, and what should you do? Discuss with the group.

E4

Did you ever have really weird feelings or sensations that made you think you were going crazy, like not knowing what was real, or seeing things? What did you do about it?

E1

Your friend tells you she (he) thinks she (he) might have venereal disease. What would you advise her (him) to do? What alternatives are there for help? Discuss this with the group.

E2

Pretend you have done some sexual things you are now ashamed of, and a "friend" has told others about it. How would you handle your embarrassment and anger? Discuss with the group.

E3

Graduation Certificates

Certificate of Graduation

This certificate will show that _____ has successfully completed a Group Course called "That Was Then, But This Is Now." This certificate will show that the above person has learned facts about abuse, that she has learned that sometimes bad things happen to good people, and that it is not ever the child's fault. She has also learned what to do if someone tries to abuse her, and understands that we all have a right to keep our bodies private. _____ knows that she is a good person, and that she has a right to be proud of herself. If something happens in the future, _____ can contact the group leaders or social worker at the following phone number: _____. The above-named person also knows how to call the police at 911. She has learned that she is a strong person, and a good person. What happened was THEN; this is NOW. _____ knows what to do to keep from being abused.

CONGRATULATIONS!

Signed _____   Date _____

K3

Certificate of Graduation

This certificate will show that _____ has successfully completed a Group Course called "That Was Then, But This Is Now." This certificate will show that the above person has learned facts about abuse, that he has learned that sometimes bad things happen to good people, and that it is not ever the child's fault. He has also learned what to do if someone tries to abuse him, and understands that we all have a right to keep our bodies private. _____ knows that he is a good person, and that he has a right to be proud of himself. If something happens in the future, _____ can contact the group leaders or social worker at the following phone number: _____. The above-named person also knows how to call the police at 911. He has learned that he is a strong person, and a good person. What happened was THEN; this is NOW. _____ knows what to do to keep from being abused.

CONGRATULATIONS!

Signed _____   Date _____

K4